The Cochise Cowboys

Who were these men?

by

Joyce Aros

GOOSE FLATS PUBLISHING   TOMBSTONE ~ ARIZONA

THE COCHISE COUNTY COWBOYS
Who Were These Men?

©2011 Joyce Aros
ISBN 978-0-9825963-4-0
Library of Congress Control Number: 2011923486

First printing November 2011
Second printing February 2012

Published by Goose Flats Publishing
P.O. Box 813
Tombstone, Arizona 85638
(520) 457-3884
www.gooseflats.com
Illustrations by Joyce Aros

Portions were originally published in the Tombstone
Times as the series, "Who Were These Men?"

INTRODUCTION

For decades since the exciting time period when western movies and cowboy heroes ruled the airwaves, both on television and on the radio stations, our rugged and manly men of the wild frontier filled our imagination with what seemed like a pretty good way to solve problems, protect gentle women, honor even the soiled doves, and maintain peace and order in a rugged and explosive environment.

We had Paladin who sold his gun but always to right wrongs; we followed the many personal stories each week with Ward Bond and his wagon train... always a satisfactory ending. There was the Lawman, the Ponderosa bunch, the Virginian, and an endless list of cool but righteous individuals. America loved it's folksy heroes and all little boys wanted to be Gene Autry or Roy Rogers. Gunsmoke with marshal Matt Dillon appealed to the more mature audience and could get quite violent in some of the earlier episodes, but western fans were now demanding a little more realism and less guitar pickin'.

And with that more sophisticated audience came the adventures of Bat Masterson, gentleman gambler, gunfighter, and lawman. Now we were getting a different look at the western hero.

However, it was the arrival on the scene of Wyatt Earp, Frontier Marshal in all his brocaded finery that truly captured the television audience's imagination. The silver brocaded vest, the watch fob, the huge Buntline Special that he used to crack the bad guys over the head...wow! It seemed to roll it all into one. Amazingly, that image has endured despite the many, many books written about Wyatt Earp and his brothers, along with their nasty sidekick, Doc Holliday. Some of these books actually exposed the Earps for the bad boys they really were. Nevertheless, no one wanted to accept such a representation of their favorite lawman, and so Wyatt will reign supreme for some time to come.

But the tide is turning; many more serious students of the old west are becoming interested in all the peripheral characters that surrounded the intriguing stories fashioned out of the lives of the heroes. These men, both friends and enemies, have stories to tell as well. Some far more interesting than the heroes. More than that, they add the color to the kaleidoscope of peoples that made up the frontier and it's myriad of adventures. They taught us more about how people lived in that time period; why some appeared to be bad when they really were only dealing with events around them, and why others appeared good when they had learned to deal with the hand dealt them and rise above it. All wore shades of grey.

This little volume is attempting to provide information that will help, hopefully, to give the interested reader a more rounded view of the men of Cochise County in the early 1880's who have since come to be known as 'outlaws.' Some clearly are not, though they bear that stigma. Others have earned the black letter, but through circumstances they often had little control over. And of course, a few were just bad boys.

So the question is asked, "Who were these men?" Were they truly criminals; rustlers, murderers, stage robbers and thieves? Let's see what you think after you read up on these few. Some have very little history to draw on, others have left a good trail. Follow their trail and see for yourself.

Joyce A. Aros
Tombstone, Arizona

APPRECIATION

No book writes itself; it comes about because of the support and encouragement the author receives from generous friends and willing researchers. I have several to thank for the help I've received. Janice Hendricks and Keith Davis have been my strongest support, devoting precious time and effort to help this book develop.

My dear friend Tom Gaumer has also contributed hours of his time to delve into the depths of historical fact and fiction and surface with wonderful little gems of information long buried for lack of interest or knowledge.

Not to be overlooked are the many persons who have patiently replied to my questions placed on several Old West discussions boards on the Internet, each having something to offer to build my own knowledge.

Joyce A. Aros
Tombstone, Arizona

ILLUSTRATIONS

TABLE OF CONTENTS

Newman "Old Man Clanton"

Chapter One

Old Man Clanton

Barely daylight creeping over the tops of the hills surrounding Guadalupe Canyon along the Mexican border, birds are beginning to move about seeking their breakfast of bugs and seeds, there are sounds of...rifle and pistol shots!

The startled men in the cow camp struggled to get out of their bedrolls, recognizing the danger with quickening adrenalin, reacting to familiar sounds of danger, yet just not fast enough.

Newman Clanton, the camp cook, fell from an almost upright position to a flat sprawl across the campfire's soft embers from the night before. Several others in the camp were also killed, young men in their prime. Only two survived the rapid onslaught of Mexican retaliation. This for a previous attack that these men would pay for with their lives, an incident in which they were not involved.

The Tombstone Daily Epitaph of August 16th, 1881, carried the particulars;

"*.... a party consisting of William Lang, Dick Gray, Jim Crane, Charlie Snow, the senior Clanton, William Byers and Harry Earnshaw camped last Friday night in Guadalupe canyon about one hundred and ten miles east of Tombstone and very near to the Mexican line.*

Early on Saturday the party was attacked by Mexicans and Lang, Gray, Crane, Snow and Clanton were killed. Byers escaped with a wound in the abdomen while Ernshaw ran away amidst a shower of bullets, one of which grazed his nose. It is estimated that the Mexican party numbered twenty-five to thirty men. The condition of the camp indicated that the attack came just as the murdered men were about getting up; one had evidently been killed while yet laying down..."

One of the more interesting observations about this episode is the lack of notoriety pertaining to the death of Newman Clanton, known in the surrounding area as 'Old Man Clanton.' Why should this catch our attention? Because from the time the Earps, the McLaurys, and the Clantons clashed a couple of months later, the legend of old man Clanton's depravations throughout the southeastern Arizona territory as a patriarch of outlaw sons and equally wicked camp followers had inundated historic writings with myths and half-truths that promoted the idea of a well organized gang of thieves, murderers and stage robbers under his control. Yet, the local papers barely mentioned his passing. In fact, they simply referred to him as 'the senior Clanton,' possibly not even knowing his full name.

But is this so? There is a mixture of reports from some responsible as well as dubious characters from those times past which might well confuse us. Perhaps it would be most interesting to examine both sides and see what comes up.

So then; who was this man? Who was old man Clanton and how did he become so controversial when so little was known about him?

Contemporary accounts, such as the above newspaper report, do not describe an outlaw king, an organized crime leader. Actually, there is very little information to be gleaned about Mr. Clanton. But what little there is, is most interesting.

Newman Clanton was a widower whose background was quite unremarkable. His past was similar to that of thousands of men, who at a young age, had struck out in wagon trains with their families for the promises of the western territories. Sometimes this took long arduous months and even years of temporary locations while health problems intervened or monies needed to be earned to press on. Relocating a family on the frontier was no easy task.

It is not necessary or advantageous to cover those years. The real interest in the development of the Clanton clan probably starts in the early 1870's in the Gila valley in the Arizona territories. Prior to that, life was fraught with hard work and disappointment. But the Gila valley held promise and Newman Clanton threw himself and his growing sons into the struggle with an aspiration he had not felt for some time. The boys were of an age to be of great value as laborers. The oldest boy with him was John Wesley, who later settled in California. Phineas, who would be about 29 in 1874, was the oldest to remain with the family. Joseph Isaac would be about 27, and young Billy would be around 12 or 13 years old. For him and his sister Mary Elsie, childhood would be far behind them.

Now the controversy begins. Mr. Clanton was attempting to start a large farming community. *The Arizona Citizen* of December 13, 1873, praised his efforts and described how he and his sons had laid claim to water, locating a line, and how the four of them had dug a ditch two and a half miles long which carried 1,880 cubic feet of water for irrigation. They literally irrigated the fields with their own sweat! A monumental task for sure. But the write-up goes on to say that the Clantons had sufficient water to irrigate a whole tract of land measuring 25,000 acres if managed properly. They had already cultivated 100 acres and were looking to sow and plant at least 600 acres. And shortly, other families were to arrive. This promised the development of a school and a church, and success at last for Newman Clanton.

But there is the controversy. A man by the name of Joseph Fish did not have such glowing things to say about the Clantons and their settlement. He claimed *"...in August of 1873, a man by the name of Clanton with four sons and a son-in-law by the name of Smith came into the valley and took up the old Hines ditch, but it does not appear that they did much. Being close to Camp Thomas, they doubtless lived as many others did around the military outposts, by doing a little something for the Government and getting about five prices for it. This was easier than to reclaim the soil which required diligent and hard labor..."*

Who this man named Joseph Fish is, no one seems to know. The record of him that I found had no references. But it's interesting to note that his comments referred to 1873, a time when the Clantons first arrived in the Gila valley. Perhaps Mr. Fish might have had a better report if he had waited and given the Clantons time to get going on their project. Nothing of such magnitude is accomplished overnight.

In 1874 Mr. Clanton submitted a petition signed by himself, his sons, and a few other farmers requesting the establishment of a precinct to be called Clantonville. Apparently no action was taken on their request. No reason has been found.

But the *Tucson Citizen* was somewhat impressed, because on September 12, 1874, they wrote a very positive report on the Clanton's efforts.

"All who live in the Gila Valley near old Camp Goodwin and at Pueblo Viejo, are enthusiastic in their accounts of the richness of the soil and the ease with which a man may make a farm. N.H. Clanton gave us these items last week but after our paper was filled. About twelve months ago he moved to a point near old Camp Goodwin and about 160 miles northeast of Tucson, and within Pima county. The place is now called Clantonville. During the year he has been there, himself and three sons have cut a ditch from the Gila river; planted 120 acres with wheat, corn, barley and all kinds of vegetables; and from nothing of consequence to start with, now has a fine farm and plenty about him. All his crops have grown nicely and some of them unusually large. Portions of his corn grew to be twelve to fourteen feet high with two large ears on a stalk. It was so nearly matured two weeks ago that scarcely an ear could be obtained soft enough for table use. He reports grass plentiful and from five to six feet in height. The cattle are fat and everything is in a fine condition. All parties east or west who desire a very fine place to make a good home easily and cheaply can not do better than to go into the Gila valley. Land is abundant at government price and the public surveys will be extended there during the present year. Anyone desiring more detailed information can get it by addressing N.H. Clanton, Camp Grant, Arizona.

Last year we gave Mr. Clanton a quart of white winter rye, which the Commissioner of Agriculture had forwarded to Hon. R.C. McCormick. He sowed it and it grew surprisingly. Fully one half was destroyed by the breaking of a ditch, yet he gathered one and a half bushels of beautiful rye. We lately gave him a few sacks of winter wheat forwarded as stated in the Citizen last week, from the Department of Agriculture. The best varieties may soon be had in abundance by carefully cultivating the seed received from Washington. The Agriculture Department distributes only the choicest kinds. A few sacks are still at the Territorial Secretary's Office."

Two conflicting reports, not unusual in the saga of the Clantons. One describes a ner-do-well bunch of hillbillies mooching off the government; and the other, what seems to be a reputable pair of newspaper reporters and the reports from government authorities, describe hard working and ambitious men, struggling to establish a society of equally determined families in a blossoming and hopeful environment. The desire of Newman Clanton to establish a school and a church speak well for the kind of man he was, a respectable family patriarch well grounded in the principle of American pioneer ideals.

But by 1877 the Clantons had given up and moved on to another section of the Arizona Territory. Clantonville, the budding paradise of the Gila valley, had failed for reasons that are yet to be uncovered. Certainly it wasn't for lack of trying on the part of Newman Clanton and his family.

And it is the next location in the San Pedro valley where the real story comes to light, the accusations of thievery and murder, and the development of an outlaw gang that terrorized the southeastern territories. How did such a change come about.....or did it?

Chapter Two

Old Man Clanton part 2

When the remnants of the Clanton family settled into a small section of southeastern Arizona territory in 1877 the area was rife with bronco Apaches and all the elements of a rough frontier existence. But the advantage was plenty of water from the San Pedro River and the Babocomari creek, and plenty of good grass and rich soil. Unlike today, the San Pedro valley was a paradise for a farmer or rancher. Once again, Newman Clanton's instincts were good, based on his farmer's savvy regarding the land and its promise. He was ready to start again; because there was no other way.

At the same time Clanton and his sons were carving out a home on the range, hand laying adobe bricks to fashion shelter and corrals, Ed Schieffelin was hurrying to Globe where he could get his find of silver ore assayed, confirming his belief that he had found a rich deposit in the hills nearby, thereby realizing his dream. As a result, in no time at all, the boomtown of Tombstone rose out of the rocky hills on Goose Flats while the Clanton ranch took shape nine miles to the southwest.

Thirty-five miles or so northwest along the Babocomari, another ranch was taking shape. The McLaury brothers were hard-working young men from New York state and who had started the growing of

7

alfalfa in the valley. They soon became fast friends with the Clanton brothers.

All the players in the Clanton saga were coming together.

The Clantons started out farming and keeping dairy cattle, and were quiet, industrious neighbors. Before too long though, they started to branch out. Phineas and Ike, the two older boys, had been freighting between the northern areas around the Gila valley and the San Pedro. Ike got enthused over the development of the Tombstone town, and branched out on a business venture. He opened the Star café, but apparently gave that up after a short time. Young Billy worked the ranch with his father and seemed to stay close to home for the most part.

But Charleston and Millville and numerous other satellite towns sprang up in response to Tombstone's explosion, and the populations of these needed beef. The local ranchers could not meet the growing need. Even the government demanded more and more supplies as the Camps all around mushroomed into Forts full of soldiers needed to protect the miners, merchant shipments, and ranchers from the Apache raids. The San Carlos Apache reservation also needed to be supplied. It was only natural that the small developing ranches looked for a way to meet the requirements of budding commerce.

And when they looked, they looked south.

Southeastern Arizona was a no-man's land of mountain ranges, valleys, and Apaches. A perfect refuge for a fluid company of young cowboys who had drifted in from Texas and New Mexico, some from farther east. John Slaughter brought a number of them with him when he drove cattle from Texas to establish a small cattle empire along the Mexican border, and a few ended up working at times for the Clanton ranch. These men banded together in loose groups, at times working the small ranches, at times occupying themselves in rustling cows from across the border, occasionally involved in smuggling and on occasion some would get together and rob a stage of its payroll shipment or bullion. If they had not been before, they rapidly became bad actors due to their nomadic lifestyle, causing a lot of problems for Cochise County.

In this vast land of great distances fraught with danger, hospitality was a given. No rancher, farmer, prospector or traveler would turn another away from his fire, food or shelter. To do so might put a man in real peril. No questions were asked; such queries would be unacceptable. As a result, every rancher hosted cowboys, rustlers, stage robbers, murderers and smugglers without knowing, and just as often with knowledge, but no words were spoken about it. The McLaurys were among the ranchers who said that no one would go hungry at their ranch. Their ranch in the Sulphur Springs Valley was at a perfect crossroads for travelers from every direction and was a frequent stop-over for posses, Cavalry and outlaws alike.

As these men came together from time to time, friendships and business arrangements developed, and soon the Clantons and McLaurys became brokers for the men who were moving cattle illegally across the border from Mexico. The enormous demands for beef were being met and the butchers, the restaurants, the government buyers, were all happy. The ranchers were making big money. And everyone's conscience was clear because no one cared that Mexicans were being robbed. The Alamo was too recent in their history.

It is from this development that the Clanton family became connected with outlawry and the whispers suggesting an organized gang surfaced, though not until after the gunfight on Fremont Street.

Around this time Mr. Clanton began to be referred to as 'Old Man Clanton,' a common designation for an older family head. It in no way carried the connotation of a gang leader or rustler chief.

But there is more controversy! The Earps and their associates along with the backing of the colorful Epitaph newspaper, edited by the equally flamboyant John Clum, had painted a picture of organized outlawry operated by such luminous and violent leaders as John Ringo, Curly Bill Brocious, and of course, Old Man Clanton!

But responsible and respected ranchers from the district didn't see it that way. Frank Shearer was one of these. He was a rancher from the Bisbee area and remembered the Clanton family very well. Mr. Shearer said that of all the ranchers and cowboys in the area, the Clantons were the best liked by everyone. Charlie Locklin, a Bisbee pioneer, described Newman Clanton as always neat and well-groomed, the boys as very handsome.

As the cattle business got bigger, Old Man Clanton established a ranch in the Animas valley, across the state line into New Mexico. Stories suggest that his purpose was to build a triangular route for the rapid dispersal of stolen cattle out of Mexico, the other two advantageous points of distribution being the McLaury ranch near Soldier Holes in the Sulphur Springs valley and the Clanton ranch run by the sons up near Lewis Springs in the San Pedro valley. But there was never any solid backing for such an assumption and Newman Clanton was never charged or substantially accused of any crime.

The boys were certainly involved in the lucrative cattle buying business and possibly in cattle rustling also, but it appears that the they were more in the line of brokers, or middlemen, as were the McLaurys. Undeniably, both families had associates and hired hands that were of bad reputations. Most of these freely raided into Mexico and supplied the much-needed beef for Cochise County and all its mining communities as well as the government that turned a blind eye in order to furnish meat for the San Carlos reservation and the numerous Forts throughout the area. Many small ranchers enlarged their herds by the same means. Few concerned themselves with the plight of Mexico or the trouble that was looming on the horizon.

Old Man Clanton was killed in 1881, just a couple of months before his youngest son, Billy. There was no development of evidence that he was an outlaw leader or head of a clan of murderous offspring. Perhaps he died too soon and the support for such narratives did not surface. But there are two accounts that surround his untimely death. The one story says that he was moving stolen cattle out of Mexico at the time of his death and paid for it with his life and the lives of his various companions. The other says that he had bought the herd of Mexican cattle and was on his way home when Mexican Rurales came across the camp and chose to retaliate against these Gringos for a previous massacre by others against Mexican citizens.

But the fact that the initial newspaper coverage lent no negative connotations to his activity at the time of his death speaks volumes. In fact, the papers did not even recognize him as anything other than a family head, referring to him as 'the senior Clanton'. There is no reason to regard the patriarch of the Clanton family as any more than what he appeared to be; a hard working farmer and rancher trying to carve a heritage for himself and his family out of a rugged and dangerous frontier, as were so many others of his time. Interestingly, that newspaper account was in none other than the *Tombstone Epitaph,* the antagonist of the cowboys in the area. Surely, if there were a connection to crime in the life of Old Man Clanton, the Epitaph would have heralded it clearly.

Chapter Three

Ike Clanton

Of all the characters involved in the Tombstone story probably no one has been as vilified as has Ike Clanton, Old Man Clanton's middle son. Joseph Isaac Clanton has borne the brunt of the criticism for the outbreak of the gunfight on Fremont Street for over 130 years and has been openly condemned for the death of his younger brother and his two close friends, the McLaury brothers. Mention Ike's name and the immediate epithets that surface are of a loud-mouthed drunken troublemaker. Nothing good is said about Ike Clanton.

Like the whole Clanton family, Ike is also surrounded in controversy. The interesting angle on the story of Ike's involvement on October 26th is that no one other than modern writers actually held Ike accountable for the trouble. At the time, Ike was not attacked in the local newspapers, there was no retaliation by local cowboys and ranchers, and no reports of bad feeling toward Ike had surfaced in personal oral history accounts. So how did this attitude develop? It appears to have started in Walter Noble Burn's well written saga about Tombstone. He called it 'an Iliad of the southwest.' Mr. Burns took real people and turned them into characters of greater depth and depravation, making them live all over again.

We can pick up Ike's story from the time of his ranching concerns in the San Pedro valley. Both he and his brother Phineas kept their interests up in the Gila valley area, Phin maintaining property up there. The two brothers worked as freighters for a while before focusing on the cattle industry. In the beginning, the Clantons were essentially farmers, working the land, keeping dairy, and turning their hand in back breaking labor at whatever would provide sustenance and covering, as did so many others in these harsh environments.

Their fortunes were limited and often fraught with failure. Starting over was a given and in those days, few complained. They just 'pulled up their bootstraps' and did what needed to be done. Isaac Clanton was not a man easily deterred. He knew nothing other than hard work, and he responded to the growing development of booming Tombstone by opening up a restaurant in the area, the Star Café. A short-lived enterprise, but an enterprise nevertheless.

One has to wonder what kind of man Ike was.....really; for he extracts such strong feelings from people who never knew him. An examination of Joseph Isaac Clanton might be very revealing, even enlightening.

There is a formal studio photograph of Ike taken around the time of the events he was involved in while in Tombstone. It shows us a very handsome man in his early thirties, smartly dressed and posed with comportment. He does not appear as the raunchy and slovenly character so often portrayed in books and films. Contemporary accounts from those who knew him seem to describe an intelligent and witty individual, apparently one who is respected and liked by his peers. Ike seemed to be a man who had an eye for business opportunities and was outgoing enough to pursue them.

Isaac Clanton has not shown either a record of excessive drinking to the point of being troublesome, nor has he shown to be cowardly at any time. Cowards would be recognized pretty quickly in Ike's environment and would be ostracized just as quick. It is fair to say most frontiersmen had little use for loud-mouthed blowhards as well. Considering the circle of associates that Ike moved in, it is hard to believe any of these attributes would be tolerated in a man that worked with ranchers as well as outlaws. Such a reputation in the town would make him the brunt of derogatory comments as well if he displayed that type of personality all the time. Logic and reason should cause us to take another look at this man. Most of the negative comments about Ike Clanton surfaced after the gunfight on Fremont Street and came from the mouths of the Earps and their cronies. In later years, Wyatt Earp's devoted fans have enlarged on this theme over the years until such viewpoints seem to have become almost fact; at least they are accepted as fact.

Yet there are substantiated reports of Ike's reckless behavior, and in those times, would it not be expected in men who lived such precarious lives? They were clearly a rough lot, with a casual attitude toward the law due to living in remote and lawless locales; certainly avoiding the towns that had strong law enforcement. Many of the outlaw element of Cochise County hung out in a town north west of Tombstone called Gayleyville, and also Charleston, a mill town to the south of Tombstone. Both these locations afforded much more freedom for such free spirits to cut loose.

But Tombstone had laws and enforcers, so Clanton & Company caused very few problems when doing business in the desert metropolis of upscale hotels, restaurants, and fancy saloons. Most problems that erupted in Tombstone were caused by the local miners and gamblers' altercations.

Ike's one or two reported rabble rousing episodes are tame when one considers the potential for danger from these types of men and also the reputations already established for pretty rough stuff. Most often quoted to show what a bad man Ike was is the hell-raising at Maxey, a town up in Graham County. It seems that Ike Clanton, along with a few other cowboys/rustlers from the Gayleyville area, had run a good-sized herd of cattle up north for sale to the quartermaster at the San Carlos reservation. As the story goes, the man refused to pay full price because he suspected the cattle were likely stolen; or he figured he could bargain because the cowboys would not want to drive the cattle all the way back to their range. Whatever the situation, the cowboys ended up selling the cattle for half the requested value and were pretty hot under the collar about it. The men involved were reported to be John Ringo, Ike Clanton and a few others from the border area. They headed out to Maxey and got roaring drunk, so they say, and apparently shot up the town and did some damage to the general store as well. One of the bunch actually shot into the window of a house in town and narrowly missed a woman in her kitchen. Drunk and stupid, the shooter probably never intended to shoot the woman or do anything other than raise a ruckus, something that was often done with guns in those days. But the incident went down against Ike Clanton for all time and those who want to disparage Ike use it as though Ike alone treed the town.

In Tombstone Ike got into an altercation with a local gambler. Some disagreement came up; the gambler struck Ike in the face. A direct challenge that Ike could not ignore. Both men, being unarmed due to the city ordinance, went to get heeled and came back to meet each other on Allen street, serious about a shootout. Virgil Earp managed to break it up and the Epitaph reported the event, not stating who caused the trouble or if either man was drunk. But from the time that article surfaced, it's been held against Ike as the instigator of that episode!

There is no record of Ike starting trouble anywhere. But he was not a man to run away from it when it showed up. Such was the case on the evening of October 25th, 1881. Ike was not the aggressor when Doc Holliday found him in a lunchroom quietly enjoying a sandwich, likely sober and also not armed. Holliday might have been drunk though there is no real support for it other than that he was known to be a heavy drinker. At any rate, the argument that Holliday started triggered a series of small events that got blown out of control, and Ike, in attempting to defend himself got caught up in a whirlwind of controversial happenings that escalated to unbelievable results.

Should Ike have been blamed for the downward spiral that led to the deaths of his brother and friends? In his day, everyone had to arbitrate their own problems and handle them immediately. The challenge by Holliday had to be met. There was no avoiding it or putting it off, not in the minds of such men. A mutual respect should prevail among these men when everyone packs a gun, but Ike was not shown that respect and he would have to vindicate himself or find another county to live in! Ike armed himself and sought out his antagonist.

Though the ensuing events were horrendous and Ike was held responsible by many today, should not much of the accountability be put on the Earps; lawmen who carried the badges, the authority, and the obligation to mete out justice in a controlled and accountable way? It was not!

After the disappointing results of the Hearing in which the Earps and Doc Holliday were exonerated, Ike moved up to the Springerville area where his brother

Phin already had property holdings. He continued in ranching and was often accused of rustling, he and Phin both. The accusations were about one calf or one steer, and newspaper reports seem to be a good year apart! It seems rather odd that men who dealt in huge amounts of cattle and money would get involved in stealing a single calf. It's difficult to build a herd that way. How true these reports are is not clear. However, Ike and Phin both were accused of a rustling activity in which Ike was pursued by a mail-order detective and killed, and Phin was arrested and sentenced to some years in Yuma prison.

Both of these happenings were very questionable. The Clanton brothers had a ranch on the New Mexico state line or just over it. There was an unfortunate shooting of a young cowboy at their ranch by a Clanton crony, Lee Renfroe, and under somewhat mysterious conditions. Renfroe got into an argument with the young man and quickly pulled a gun, shooting the boy dead. Ike was in the room at the time and seemed to be too shocked by the unexpected action to respond in time. However, the two brothers helped Renfroe to escape from the ranch, feeling that he was a friend of theirs and they should aid him. The dead man's father was a powerful and wealthy man in the district and pressure was brought against the Clanton brothers from that time on. The reports of stolen cattle associated with the Clantons and their brother-in-law, Ebin Stanley, multiplied in a short time, and it would appear as though their final situation was a put-up job. Certainly Phin was railroaded, as the man who testified against him later confessed to the false testimony and Phin was released from prison. If Ike was hunted and killed by Detective Brighton, also an associate of the false witness, for the same charge, then the shooting of Ike Clanton was actually a murder.

Though Ike was a rugged individual, certainly a tough frontiersman, his tragic background haunted him to the end. His father was gunned down in August of 1881 and shortly thereafter, in October, his younger brother Billy was murdered before his eyes on Fremont Street in Tombstone. After Billy's death, the two remaining brothers went out to the Guadalupe Canyon area where their father was buried; dug up his remains and transported his body to Tombstone to be buried next to Billy. A sad and unpleasant act of love, one that must have meant a great deal to them.

The two events had a profound effect on Ike. The exoneration of the killers and the disheartening events that followed left him a broken man. He became a heavy drinker and often a troublesome character around Apache and Graham Counties. What we recognize as depression today would have been considered morose and sullen behavior at that time.

Though Ike Clanton is today looked upon as a pariah in the Tombstone saga, yet among his peers, lawful and lawless, Ike was not viewed as such. He was recognized for what he was; simply a product of his times and circumstances.

Author's notes: It is necessary to mention an incident in which Ike and his younger brother Billy were said to have been involved in which certainly questions the character of both men. However, it is important to note that the account is oral history, the recollections of a man who lived in the area and who claimed to know that Ike and Billy Clanton were both involved in a massacre of Mexican smugglers in the Skeleton Canyon area, a favorite trade route. Without any corresponding support I am reluctant to accept the story as reliable, but nevertheless, felt it was something to be offered in the record. Perhaps further evidence will surface. Up to this time, I have found nothing in the Clanton boys' history to suggest they were wanton killers, though they probably rustled cattle from across the border, as did so many other ranchers and cowboys trying to deal with economic survival on the frontier in the nineteenth century.

Chapter Four

Billy Clanton

The story of the Clanton family is not unique to the southwestern frontier. Life was dangerous and fraught with daily struggles for the necessities, and few families escaped misadventure. Pioneer diaries and lovingly preserved letters are full of the adversities of the westward push to start a new life over fresh horizons. For the Clantons, like so many others, the loss of loved ones under difficult circumstances was all a part of their narrative.

We know little about young Billy Clanton except for his unfortunate part in the shooting tragedy in Tombstone in which he lost his life. The general consensus from the many books about this account is that Billy was a young tough, a wanna-be gunman who hung out with hard-core thieves, murderers and rustlers. Little sympathy is extended toward a nineteen or twenty year old cowboy who bled out his life in agony on a cold and windy afternoon on Fremont Street. Surely, he must have been looking for trouble?

But for William Harrison Clanton, it didn't matter anymore. Billy's life had been typical of the times. He lost his mother when he was four years old and had to look to his sisters, not much older than himself, for comfort and care. The father and older brothers were working from sunup to sundown and Billy would just have to grow up by himself. His two sisters didn't have it much better. The family changed locations several times from then on and each time offered hope of something better, but then, the inevitable disappointment.

By the time they settled in the Gila Valley area in Arizona Territory, the youngsters were maturing into capable survivors. The two girls had already married in California, and Billy was farming and becoming a ranch hand. Records show that he was also attending a Catholic school at the time, so clearly, it was important to Mr. Clanton that his boys get some education. Later records show that his older brother Ike was quite articulate in matters requiring correspondence both personal and business oriented. What kind of scholar Billy was, we don't know, but we can know that he was well liked by his peers.

Bill Oury tells of attending school in Tucson about 1877, remembering the Clantons at the time. His recollection was of a tough ranching family that had settled along the San Pedro and *"....Old Man Clanton feared nothing; his two boys, Ike and Bill were of the same stamp. At the time I speak of, 1877-78, they were decent youngsters who came to Tucson from their father's ranch to attend school. I was younger than they were, but as they were my schoolmates, I remember them...."* Clearly Ike would have been too old to be attending school in that year, but the recollections of the persons Oury describes are probably of Billy and his sister, as that is the correct time period for Billy. At any rate, Oury seemed to remember the details quite well; *"....the boys were encouraged in manly games and sports. We used to ride horses bareback at full tilt, and pick up a handkerchief on the ground. Sometimes we fell. We used to ride bucking calves with only a leather thong lashed about the animal's middle to hold to. I've never seen youngsters do these things anywhere else.....*" Mr. Oury added, *"...it was not until after the opening of the mines in Tombstone that the Clanton boys came into notoriety. Bill was killed there in Tombstone by Wyatt Earp, his brothers, and Doc Holliday. I never knew what became of Ike...."* Interestingly, another woman who attended the same school and left her earlier record with the *Arizona Historical Society* in the memoirs of Mrs. Kitt, tells of Ike and Phin being decent youngsters at the time. There was some good child rearing by Mr. Clanton as all the boys were well liked.

So we are introduced to a boy in school, growing up on a ranch with all the hardships attached, yet enjoying some of the good experiences that a fifteen year old boy would with his schoolmates. For a ranch kid, Billy's life seemed normal.

Other contemporary accounts describe Billy Clanton as a hard-working and extremely capable cowboy, being very much appreciated during round-ups in the Sulphur Springs Valley. *(thanks to Roy Young's research)* He is referred to as a typical fun-loving and friendly young man; indeed, all the Clanton boys were spoken of as very affable. None of this fits the derogatory descriptions that surfaced *after* the Fremont Street fight.

Though the modern view of Billy is that he spent his time rustling cattle from across the border and bushwhacking Mexicans, it seems the Census record shows he spent part of 1880 in Pima County working the mines. Why would a free-wheeling young outlaw spend time working under the most merciless conditions in the mines for three or four dollars a day when he could trot across the border, shoot a couple of peons, and drive some cash-on-the-hoof back up home and make real money? Why, too, was he employed by his father to milk cows and deliver milk? Such accusations of outlawry have no concrete substance to them but do help to justify the actions of the Earps in the minds of many. So far, Billy seems to be a young cowboy older than his years due to the hard life he lived, but a legitimate rancher who had a wide range of associates.

To get a complete picture, perhaps we should take a look at Billy's circle of friends. After all, Billy was not a cherubic-cheeked innocent. Life on the frontier would never allow that.

Aside from his older brothers, Phin and Ike, and along with his father, Billy seemed to favor the company of Frank McLaury. We'll talk about the McLaury brothers soon, but they too seemed to be much maligned *after* the Fremont Street fight. Billy had still been working at a ranch up near the Gila valley in the mid seventies when Frank McLaury came by looking for work. He was hired and he and Billy worked together a while. They struck up a close and genuine friendship that lasted until their deaths, despite the difference in age. It would appear Billy could hold his own among the older men he ran with. In fact, all of these men were reputed to be expert gunmen as well as tough frontiersmen. A well respected Arizona pioneer, Frank J. Vaughn, remarked in an interview that he knew the Clantons and McLaurys well. About Billy, he said this; *"...Well, Billy Clanton was the quickest man with a gun I have ever seen. He could ride full speed past four or five cans, turn quickly, shoot from the hip, and hit every one of them..."*

Billy's favorite stomping ground was Charleston, only two or three miles from his home ranch. It was a lively town and harbored some notorious characters from time to time. Young Clanton hung out with the likes of Curly Bill Brocious, John Ringo, Pony Diehl, Frank Stilwell, the Patterson brothers and a host of others. Billy kept rough company, but then, in his line of work, there wasn't any other kind. His father and brothers were just as tough.

At the Hearing in which the Earps and Holliday were examined regarding the murders of Billy and the McLaurys, witnesses testified that Billy was considered among the finest gunmen in the territory, so it is reasonable to assume he was more than capable of keeping up with the men he associated with. Yet Billy Clanton was never arrested, accused, or charged with any crime. The incident regarding Wyatt Earp's race horse has so many versions that it is impossible to get a true picture as to whether Billy actually came across the horse or really stole it. Stealing such a well-known horse does not seem to make much sense. Billy was not unacquainted with the horses in the area. People knew others' horses the same way cars are recognized today.

Then what are we to think of a young rancher who is well-liked, hard-working, never in trouble with the law but well acquainted with all the known outlaws in the territory? Only that Billy Clanton moved among the people that were available to him in the environment he worked in. That he enjoyed the excitement and adventure had to be a given; he was young and the opportunity was there. But was he a hardened criminal defying the law at every opening? Hardly! Billy was gunned down in the street in Tombstone because he was with his brother and friends who had a personal complication with the Earp brothers that they themselves were not sure of. One can only feel anguish for this young cowboy as he fell back against the little house from the impact of .45 slugs tearing into his chest, his wrist smashed from another bullet and his life ebbing away as he struggled to fight back to the last bullet despite the shock and confusion. Surely if there could have been a courageous hero in such a bloody and shameful confrontation that day, it was twenty year old Billy Clanton.

William Lloyd Claiborne

Chapter five

Billy Claiborne

Billy Claiborne was a young man who is often viewed as a peripheral character in the Tombstone saga. There is little understanding of who he was or where he fit in. He was a cowboy, but he also worked at mining, driving freight, and whatever else he could to turn a dollar as did most in the southeastern Arizona territory. He was young and on his own on the frontier; a dangerous place to be, far from home and hearth.

The desert country was full of young men like him who struck out for adventure and independence, but were also often forced to start a man's job at a very young age and as a result, felt they'd earned their spurs prematurely. Perhaps our young Vaquero fits this category.

Young Claiborne's background is rather unremarkable when one considers that almost all these cowboys grew up in the upheaval of the post-Civil War atmosphere. Their homes were uprooted, their families often scattered or killed, and survival became a daily routine. Hard times breed hard men, and these youngsters developed a thick hide very quickly.

Like many of that time, Billy left home in his teens to work as a wrangler for a cattle driving outfit. The wrangler was a step above the cook's helper, caring for the 'Remuda' of horses for the many cowboys on the ranch. Each hand might have access to up to ten horses for his use, having two or three horses in his string that were specialized. For example, a horse that had a good walk, covering a lot of ground quickly and smoothly would be the choice of a cowboy who had to do line-riding; checking the miles of fences that were starting to go up in some ranching areas at the time, or checking on the scattered water holes. Several of a rider's animals might be his 'brush-poppers,' horses that would not hesitate to charge through pretty rough country in chasing the half-wild cattle that needed to be roped, branded and worked back into the herd. The wrangler had a huge responsibility, but it was a step forward in his education as a working cowboy.

All of this helped to build Billy's reputation as a hard worker and dependable man 'to ride the river with,' a high regard indeed from fellow workers, who also began referring to him as "the kid" due to his short stature.

But Billy Claiborne is best remembered for his early demise at the hands of Buckskin Frank Leslie, one of the territory's more colorful characters and a deadly adversary. Whatever possessed the boy to press an issue with such a man? How did he go from being a shy, hard-working wrangler to a young man feeling capable of taking on one of Tombstone's most dangerous shootists?

Our cowboy's seasoning came about by working with some pretty rough men. He worked for John Slaughter, a Texas cowman driving a huge herd to the San Pedro valley in Arizona territory, and who had some tough cowboys in his employ. Life on a cattle drive was one way for a young man to grow up fast as there were many dangers. One would face swollen rivers, difficult cattle, ornery horses, men with little patience for greenhorns, droughts and dust storms, and the never-ending loneliness of having left family behind. What we often refer to as the "school of hard knocks!"

Having arrived in the Charleston area of the San Pedro valley, Billy continued to work for a while for Slaughter, but then moved on to a job in the mining industry, a better paying position. There was plenty of opportunity to advance at the Tombstone Mining & Milling Company, and Billy did just that. Working for Dick Gird, a friend of Slaughter's, Claiborne started out at the lower end as a rock crusher but soon climbed up the ladder until he was a smelter operator, all this in a short period of time.

One would think he would have been satisfied with such an accomplishment, but like many young trailblazers of his time, something always beckoned him to try something else and so he moved on from one job to another, never drifting too far away from his friends on the Slaughter ranch, they being like family to him. Whatever else he turned his hand at; it was for sure difficult and demanding work. Nothing came easy on the frontier.

Billy's associates were men like himself, mostly cowboys and ranchers who also turned to other jobs from time to time to stir up a little cash. Freighting, hiring out to other ranchers during round-ups, even at times working the mines. And for a little rest and recreation, the lively town of Charleston was beckoning. Billy developed friendships with the Clanton boys, the McLaurys and a few others that were of notoriety in the area. Charleston was a town that let the men blow off steam, as there was little in the way of law enforcement, if any. All the boys looked forward to hanging out in the saloons, playing cards, visiting the girls and touching bases with each other as they were often scattered in different directions.

Phin Clanton had a small house in town and the story goes that Billy and others often stayed there when in Charleston. The Clantons, McLaurys, some of the crowd from the San Simon region and Gayleyville, often collected in Charleston rather than Tombstone. It was much more to their liking as they were cowboys, not professional gamblers and businessmen such as frequented the larger town.

But anywhere and anytime in this rugged neighborhood, trouble could surface without warning and without reason. In a time when everyone carried a weapon, each had to show a mutual respect so that there would not be explosive eruptions. On a day in October of 1881, Billy Claiborne was making the rounds in Charleston, visiting friends in the saloons, as was the custom for cowboys in town. But a man by the name of James Hickey had been drinking excessively for several days and apparently making a general nuisance of himself. He singled out Billy for his particular brand of attention and harassed him mercilessly, following him around the town, insisting on buying Billy a drink at each saloon though Billy declined over and over. The strain between the two developed into an argument and Hickey began abusing Billy with slurs regarding his manhood and his "Billy the Kid" nickname. When Hickey finally pulled a gun, Billy could take no more, pulling his gun and shooting the obnoxious drunk in the head and killing him.

Billy Claiborne turned himself over to the local Constables and an inquest was held almost immediately. Testimony from eyewitnesses showed that Hickey had continually provoked the young cowboy, using very foul language and advancing on the boy, though Billy cautioned him several times to leave him alone as he backed away, brandishing his pistol in warning. Hickey only became more offensive.

There was no jail in Charleston so Billy was moved to Tombstone to await a hearing. His friends, the Clantons and McLaurys posted his bond and he was out until a bail hearing to be held on October 25th. While awaiting the court date, he worked out on the range south of Tucson in order to avoid further trouble.

Billy returned to Tombstone on October 25th and happened to run into Ike Clanton and Tom McLaury who had just come into town to do some business. The story goes that the two friends paid the additional fine that was charged to Billy. It is likely they spent some time together the rest of the afternoon and evening prior to Ike's late night run-in with Doc Holliday, but that is only a reasonable assumption. Clearly our young man's life is going to get more complicated in a matter of hours.

On the 26th of October, the day of the gunfight that went down in Tombstone's history, Claiborne had run into Tom and Ike again, escorting them to the doctor for their head wounds. He tagged along until he connected up with his friend Billy Clanton who had just come into town and was looking for his brother, Ike. In a matter of little more than half an hour, Billy Claiborne saw his friends shot down on Fremont Street and was spared the same fate only because Sheriff Behan shoved him into a doorway to protect him.

Billy's reaction to the shooting of Hickey by immediately turning himself in shows that he was not a young tough with a wanton urge to kill. The times he lived in and their influence on the thinking of such men has to be considered. By the same token, it would be fair to say that Billy was completely traumatized by the murder of his friends whom he had just been standing talking with. It appears that young Claiborne took to rather heavy drinking after that experience. He was exonerated in the death of Hickey and headed up north to Globe for a while to work the mines. At some point he connected up with the John Ringo/Curly Bill crowd in the San Simon area and ended up on a drinking spree with Ringo for a while. They parted for some reason and Ringo was later found dead, an apparent suicide.

During another of Billy's excessive drinking bouts, he went too far. Frank Leslie was tending bar at the Oriental saloon in Tombstone and enjoying a good and lively political discussion with a patron when Billy came in and rather rudely injected himself into the conversation. Leslie suggested Billy 'take it outside' as he was out of line at the moment. Billy became obnoxious and stomped off fully offended. For whatever reason, he felt he could handle the situation with violence and came back gunning for Leslie with a rifle. Calling Leslie out, Billy stood on the corner near the entrance to the saloon and waited for his adversary. Leslie, clearly a cool man in a bad situation, simply picked up his pistol, stepped out the side door and shot twice, hitting the boy fatally. Billy got off one awkward shot into the dirt and collapsed. He lived long enough to be taken into the doctor and, with his dying breath, accused Leslie of murdering Ringo the day they were all drinking in that area. Frank Leslie coldly went back to his political discussion and was cleared of any charges.

Much of the record of William Claiborne shows a hard working and law-abiding cowboy and mill worker. Strong men like John Slaughter along with his wife maintained a definite fondness and respect for Billy. The boy held a number of jobs that required diligence and responsibility. Though some of his friends were rustlers, there's no record of his being involved in cattle rustling. What cowboy of the times didn't know other cowboys, both lawful and lawless?

When Billy was released on bail, he attempted to stay away from trouble by working far out on the range until his court date. Tom Thornton, who owned a hotel, said that Billy had worked for him and was a quiet, inoffensive fellow. He also made it clear, though, that the young man would defend himself when necessary.

Billy Claiborne made one fatal mistake; one he could not outgrow with time. He attempted to challenge the one man in town who would not cut him any slack despite his condition or his youth.

But hard times breed hard men...and Arizona territory was not the place to try out your mettle. Like many a young cowboy of his time, Billy didn't live long enough to develop into whatever he might have been. The old west was littered with the bodies of young men, reckless with confidence in themselves, whose lives ended prematurely. For most, their families would never know what happened to them, as the "unknown" markers on graves were everywhere. For some, it would be the unfortunate accident out on the range and a lonely grave; but for Billy, it was a cold and heartless delivery of a bullet that left his story unfinished.

Phineas Fay Clanton

Chapter Six

Phin Clanton

I wish to recognize the research efforts of both Rita Ackerman and Ben Traywick. Thanks to these generous and diligent excavators, writers like myself are able to find those little gems of information that help us to get a better picture of so many of our interesting frontier characters.

The continuing hundred and thirty year effort to paint the Clantons as the nineteenth century Dillinger gang has begun to fall flat at last. As more and more is learned about the interesting characters of southeastern Arizona territory, a better understanding of what constitutes a bad man has surfaced.

Among the men who have often been referred to as an outlaw is Phineas Fay Clanton, the older but quieter brother. Though there was an older Clanton son who moved to California and stayed there when he married, we will not find it necessary to discuss him, as he was not a part of the territorial story that brought the Clanton name to the fore.

But our Phin Clanton is a bit of a mystery man as there is very little mention of him in the various historical archives. His name floats in and out with little description of who or what he was, but we can glean a few things, and by doing so, another Clanton added to the story helps us to get a truer picture of the Clanton family as a whole.

Though Ike seemed to be outgoing and confident, and Billy seemed to be a fun-loving but hard working young cowboy, Phin leaves us little to build on. Perhaps because he was much older than his brothers, he appeared to go his own way, independent of the family unit. While the rest of the family lived and worked the ranch on the San Pedro not far from Charleston, it has been reported than Phin owned a home in the town. What he was doing there as a full time town dweller has never been established. Most of his endeavors were built around livestock. Some records show that Old Man Clanton purchased a saloon in Charleston for a short while and one wonders if Phin was perhaps running it for his father.

Independently motivated, Phin had put in a claim for land meant for himself in the northeastern section of Arizona as early as 1879; up along the New Mexico state line, an area known as the Cienega Amarilla. He established the ranch at that time, having claimed 160 acres, and built a house and corrals, thus settling in for permanent residency.

As Phin spent much of the turbulent Tombstone years at his ranch, it helps clear up the mystery as to why we know so little about him. But his name surfaces often enough to convince us that he moved back and forth rather regularly, therefore keeping close connection with his father and brothers.

Phin's name pops up several times as a participant in a sheriff's posse, and though it was not unusual for lawmen to pick capable and hardy types for such duty, much is made of the fact that Sheriff Behan used such men as the Clantons, McLaurys and others for the tough work of hunting Apaches and stage robbers. The local store clerks and barbers were less inclined for any number of reasons, and were less accustomed to long days in the saddle, sleeping on hard, rocky desert floor, and most importantly, were not very handy with six guns as to skill or determination. The Earps' posses were often made up of men who swung from one side of the law to the other, yet it bothered neither the Earps nor their later fans. But Phin Clanton and his associates were known to be tough outdoorsmen who could deal with anything that came up out there.

There are occasional comments as to the character and personality of Phineas Clanton. All seem to be favorable. Endicott Peabody, the Episcopalian divinity student who built an impressive church in Tombstone that still stands today, was a very observant man who had much to say in his diaries about the denizens of Tombstone. Though some were rather amusing, others even a little caustic, his short evaluation of Phin Clanton is interesting. The brief summary says this; *"...Phin Clanton breakfasted at table next to me. Rather a good natured looking chap..."* It is slim, but telling.

When one considers the rugged life of frontiersmen such as the Clantons and their associates, Phineas Clanton led a pretty quiet and uneventful life by comparison. He always seemed to be on the fringes and arriving a day late. He was not around when his father was murdered in Guadalupe Canyon; he was not in town when his kid brother Billy was murdered, and he was in jail when his younger brother Ike was also murdered. Did I say he led an uneventful life? But we cannot sell him short because he was a quieter, steadier man. He was as tough as the other men in his family, leading essentially the same existence. He worked cattle, as they did, no enterprise for store clerks. In fact, he lost a thumb on his right hand and part of a thumb on his left hand from dally roping cattle. But there were no counselors or physical therapists in those days and a days' work was not to be lost. There would be no real sympathy either; the response from fellow cowboys would be, "It's a long way from your heart!"

It was recorded in some oral history accounts that Phin, a Civil War veteran, was a crack shot with a rifle. It was said that when Phin went hunting for deer or other game, he only took one bullet as he never missed.

If there is truth to such a story, it would explain why Billy was such a good shot; his older brother coached him well.

Phin did not stay around the Tombstone area for long after his father and brother were killed. His home was in Apache County, and so was his sister, Mary Elsie, whom he seemed to be close to. He and her husband, Ebin Stanley, were fast friends also. Ebin Stanley was a man of good reputation and well liked in the area, but he soon became embroiled in controversy regarding some stolen cattle, and many writers have suggested that that good man was badly corrupted by his close association with the Clanton brothers. But could there be another side to the story?

There are a number of short newspaper pieces that bring out the many accusations against the Clanton brothers and Ebin Stanley regarding cattle stealing up in Graham and Apache counties. However, there are some logical questions that arise if one thinks about it. Ike Clanton and a few of his associates were frontier bankers and cattle brokers for many of the ranchers in the southeastern part of the territory, and most likely for many of the rustlers that picked up cattle belonging to Mexico. They dealt in huge sums of money through these deals. Yet, Ike and Phin were accused several times of stealing one cow or one calf. One? And a year apart! That makes no sense at all. What was the point? Why take such a risk? And Ebin Stanley had never been a cattleman, so why would he be involved in stealing one calf or one cow? How do you build a herd like that?

But there it is, in the local papers. 1883, and Phin, Ebin Stanley, even Phin's sister were accused of cattle stealing along with Ike Clanton, John Lee, J.A. Rudd and John Gibbs. From then on there were occasional accusations of wrongdoing but nothing ever stuck. The Deputy County Treasurer was robbed at gunpoint in the middle of the night and accused Ike and Phin and Ebin of the crime. However, the charges were later dropped when the real thief was caught and sent to prison. It would appear that people could be arrested and indicted quite easily in those days, the needed evidence being gathered later rather than sooner.

A young rancher by the name of Isaac Ellinger was killed at the Clanton ranch by a friend of the Clantons, Lee Renfro. It appeared to be a personal dispute over some ranch land and the matter was settled violently. Unfortunately, the Clanton boys felt the need to remain loyal in the matter to Renfro and they assisted his getaway. Strangely enough, neither one of the Clanton brothers were called as witnesses during the investigation. But the father of the murdered young man was a powerful stockman in the area and from then on the Clanton brothers were in his sights. Regular attempts to have them indicted for one crime or another ensued and Phin ended up in jail at the time that Ike was murdered. However, it was established that Phin was railroaded by a false witness and he was later released. Interestingly, the man who falsely testified against Phin was a close associate of the man who killed Ike. It has all the earmarks of a conspiracy.

Once home again, Phin led a rather ordinary life from then on. He raised goats, filed a few mining claims which amounted to nothing and married a woman with a young son. He had lost everything and had to start over, in spite of being in his fifties, and in poor health due to his short prison term.

Our quiet and sensible Clanton brother died of pneumonia after a sickness brought on by being caught in a snowstorm. He had lived a life of sorrow and heartache along with all the hardships the frontier of the 1870's and 80's had to offer. Though his name will forever be associated with outlawry and cattle rustling, no matter how unfair or unsupported, his plain grave marker is inscribed with a sentiment that shows the deep love and respect of someone who knew him well. His stepson had his gravestone marked thus..."*Not all good men wore badges...*"

Chapter Seven

The Brothers McLaury

The two men lay stretched out in the dirt on Fremont Street, their life's blood slipping out of gaping wounds. The one in the middle of the street had died instantaneously, before he hit the ground, a bullet smashing into his head. The other man lay in the dust over at the corner of Third Street, just a little west of the Fremont Street corner. He was still breathing ever so slightly, little air bubbles forming from the huge destruction of his upper torso. He could not see his brother lying across the street; he could not speak.

These men were the handsome and hard working McLaury brothers, Frank and Tom, local ranchers who had come to town to do business with nearby butchers and merchants as they had many times before.

But this time, something went terribly wrong and they were gunned down on a cold and windy afternoon by lawmen who visualized an enormous threat from these two cowboys and their young companions. This terrible scene was the result of the shoot-out just behind the OK Corral in Tombstone, Arizona Territory in 1881.

The newspaper of the day, *The Daily Nugget*, on October 27th, 1881 had this to say;

"....Of the McLaury brothers we could learn nothing of their previous history before coming to Arizona. The two brothers owned quite an extensive ranch on the lower San Pedro, some seventy or eighty miles from the city, to which they had removed their cattle since the recent Mexican and Indian troubles. They did not bear the reputation of being of a quarrelsome disposition, but were known as fighting men, and had generally conducted themselves in a quiet and orderly manner when in Tombstone..."

"...we could learn nothing...?"

How interesting! The Earp faction, including John Clum, editor of the rival voice, *The Tombstone Epitaph*, had long referred to the *Tombstone Nugget* as the voice of the Cowboys, aka local outlaws. Yet this paper had little information about them. The article states that the paper apparently attempted to investigate and learn something about the brothers and could not; yet later, the Earps and their supporters claimed these men were notorious outlaws. A bit of an enigma, wouldn't one think?

But what can *we* learn about them? How can *we* understand their sudden and violent death when they left behind a reputation of being quiet and orderly men whenever in town?

Fortunately, many of the McLaury relatives today have taken a deep interest in their infamous ancestors and have compiled family records, letters and stories that give us a more complete picture of these two young pioneers; contemporary records of the time have filled in the gaps for us.

The McLaury brothers had been raised in a fine family of Scottish-Irish background. In the Old Country, the family was known to have raised prime sheep. In the New World, they were predominately known to be lawyers and judges. Both Frank and Tom had started out toward developing a career in law, reportedly having been first or second year law students. However, as in any life story, events changed the direction of the young men and they set out on a life of adventure and independence. The West was calling!

In 1878 the boys arrived in Fort Worth, Texas along with older brother Will McLaury and his new family. Whether the two had come with Will from the Dakota Territory or joined him in Texas is not definite. But at any rate, Frank and Tom, now 28 and 23 years old, likely felt less inclined to go back to school. They struck out for Arizona Territory where there were great opportunities for adventurous and hard-working young pioneers. There are stories that indicate they traveled to Arizona on a cattle drive for either John Slaughter or John Chisum. Either way, they ended up in the Camp Thomas district of the Gila valley, a place rife with new settlers and prospects for the future.

Finding work was the first order of the day and Frank found a short-term position on the old Clanton farm which was then owned by Melvin Jones. It was here that Frank became acquainted with young Billy Clanton. Though his father had sold the farm, it seems Billy, only 16 or 17 at the time, was reluctant to leave the area and remained working for the new owner for some time. He and Frank became fast friends and it was through the Clantons that the McLaury boys became connected with so many other ranchers and cowboys when they resettled along the Babocomari creek, a tributary of the San Pedro River that ran all the way down through the southern parts of Arizona territory. The Clantons established a ranch in the same area along the San Pedro.

During this early time in the Gila valley, Frank had also assisted Melvin Jones, at that time a local Constable in law enforcement. This is interesting as it gives us an initial look at the character of Frank McLaury. Some soldiers from Camp Thomas had stolen some harness from the military when they were discharged, and the local judge had told Jones to round up the culprits and hand them over to the Camp Thomas authorities. The judge also told Jones to take one good man with him. Jones chose Frank McLaury.

The results showed that Jones had chosen well. When the two law representatives caught up with the renegades, their lives were threatened and the soldiers attempted negotiations. The soldiers also attempted to bribe Jones and McLaury, each offering $25.00 to the lawmen to buy their flight. Frank McLaury was incensed, according to Melvin Jones, and would have none of it under any circumstances. Jones told the felons that he and Frank would return to the camp and get a company of soldiers to hunt them down. The thieves finally gave themselves up and were returned to the civil court as they had requested; Jones and McLaury using discretion as lawmen often do.

So what do we learn about one of the McLaury brothers here? Apparently he was a man of integrity, at least at that time. Conversations attributed to Frank later on indicate the same attitude. It is only *after* the killings that words are put into Frank and Tom's mouths that make them appear to be desperados. These words are put there by the Earps and should certainly be considered to be self-serving, as the Earps desperately needed to make these brothers look bad in order to justify a questionable police action that resulted in the death of these two ranchers.

These young men were ambitious and diligent. At the Babocomari ranch, they farmed alfalfa hay, the first to do so in the area. Such an enterprise did not come about easily. It required long hours at hard labor, requiring also the need for irrigation ditches to be dug. They began raising cattle and horses, and later relocated to the Sulphur Springs valley, an area flush with water and good grazing.

Oral accounts show that the two brothers were well respected among their ranching neighbors, and that Tom McLaury served his neighbors as a frontier banker, loaning monies and handling financial matters in town for them. Tom was considered the harder working of the two, but that could be because he was also the quieter of the two. Perhaps he talked less and worked more. Clearly, Tom McLaury was liked and respected among his fellow ranchers and cowboys.

Stories abound of their connections with the outlaws and rustlers in the territory and some are likely true. But nothing is ever that simple. Were these two actually outlaws or rustlers themselves? It seems hard to believe that they would be so accepted by their neighbor ranchers if they were dangerous outlaws. On the day of the famous gunfight, the Clantons and the McLaury brothers were in town to close a deal for 600 head of cattle that they and their neighbor, a rancher named Frink, had rounded up and merged for a large cattle deal. Major Frink was a respected businessman with no taint to his name. It is unlikely he would collaborate with known thieves in a business consolidation. These stories simply do not stand up to reason and close scrutiny.

Many other fabrications of the Earps that suggest the McLaurys were desperados also do not stand up to honest examination. Frank Vaughn, a respected and important citizen of the southeastern Cochise County area, defended the McLaurys. This is what he had to say about them. *"...the McLaurys were as fine men as you would wish to know, not schooled but educated; if anyone in Arizona had a College degree in those days, they kept it to themselves. They were not cattle rustlers but ranchmen and owned and operated two ranches, one on the Babocomari and one in the Sulphur Springs valley near the Mule mountains...all of this written about the McLaurys is bosh...Burns, for instance, if you figured up the time, would make one of the boys a criminal at the time he was born...some day I want to write about the McLaury brothers for they have been very much misrepresented...they were educated gentlemen and came from fine people...the boys here were not cattle rustlers but regular cattlemen, and I know that ___McLaury knew too much about the killing of Bud Philpot to suit the Earps..."*

Accusations of threats against the Earps over a period of a year make absolutely no sense. Whenever the Earp brothers repeated reports of threats, they were always from people who were never asked to come forward and back up those claims. All of Virgil's complaints against the brothers were supposedly given by people in confidence, never overheard, and Virgil usually could not remember who the reporter was. Yet despite these threats of murder and mayhem, the Earps seemed not to be in fear as they felt quite comfortable accepting the McLaury brothers' hospitality at their ranch just a couple of weeks before the shootout. They also enjoyed the company of Curly Bill Brocious and a couple of his friends at the same time, Virgil shaking Bill's hand warmly and spending time chatting with him in a friendly manner; this according to *George Parsons,* a well-known crony of the Earps. Virgil also played cards most of the night before the day of the fight with Tom McLaury, Ike Clanton, and Johnny Behan, showing no evidence of being concerned for his life nor was he too disgusted for the camaraderie of a poker game with these same men.

One has to wonder where the threat was and if it existed, and why, if murder was the intent, the cowboys couldn't pull off an assassination attempt in the year prior to the gunfight with the Earps. One has to be very suspicious of the candor of the Earp brothers.

When Tom McLaury came into Tombstone, he rode in with Ike Clanton in a spring wagon for the purpose of getting supplies, as Tom, Frank, the Clantons and Major Frink had been working cattle for many days. The two men turned in their guns at the West End corral and headed into town. Neither man caused any trouble while there. The trouble started when Ike went into the Alhambra saloon to get a lunch about 1:00 am and was accosted by Doc Holliday who challenged him to a fight. Ike told him he was not armed and Doc told him to get heeled so that the next time he saw him, he would be ready to fight. Ike attempted to oblige Doc, got his rifle and his gun later on, and went looking for Doc. He didn't find him but the Earps found Ike on the street, beat him and arrested him, then took him to court to be fined for carrying arms on the street. There was more trouble in the court due to the short-fused Earps prodding Ike to fight. When Ike left the court, he headed for the gun shop to rearm.

In the meantime, Wyatt Earp left the courtroom, ran into Tom McLaury, and beat up the unarmed man quite severely. Now there are two injured men who have not initiated any trouble, Ike only retaliating.

As pre-arranged, Billy Clanton and Frank McLaury, along with Major Frink have just ridden into town to sell the cattle and meet their brothers. They were informed of the brothers' trouble the minute they got off their horses, so they did not turn in their guns as they intended to locate their brothers and get out of town before there could be any more trouble.

But they got trouble anyway. Townspeople who had observed the arrest of Ike Clanton and the beating of Tom McLaury assumed that there was more to come and began to broadcast an impending fight. While the cowboys made preparation to finish up their business and head out of town, the Earps, already in an aggressive fighting mode, were stirred up by the excited busybodies who wanted to see some action. Reports of threats were enlarged upon and were flying left and right. The Marshal, Virgil Earp, did nothing to calm the situation but rather than disperse the growing crowd, he played right into their hands and gathered his forces for a fight.

While Frank McLaury was talking with the sheriff and the rest of the boys were waiting on Ike's team and wagon to be hitched, the Earps, along with Doc Holliday, descended on the small group at a fast pace, almost running over sheriff Behan who attempted to interfere with any possible gunplay.

Though the ranchers said they did not want to fight, and a number of witnesses stated that they put their hands up when told to, still three of them were dead in seconds.

The Earp faction told their story and many witnesses gave their version of the slaughter, but the controversy rages on as to whether the lawmen were justified or not.

But perhaps the best statement regarding these two brothers was given by John Pleasant Gray, a neighboring rancher who knew them well, as did Major Frink, their business partner. Gray wrote in his book, *"When All Roads Lead To Tombstone"* this summary of the McLaury brothers; *"....these boys were plain, good-hearted, industrious fellows. They may have harbored passing rustlers at their ranch, but what rancher did not? And it would have been little of a man who would have turned away any traveler in that land of long trails and hard going....*"

Frank McLaury himself had said that no man would go hungry at his ranch. Certainly the Earp posse didn't!

Chapter Eight

Johnny Ringo

No place in the western hemisphere is there a collection of names as stimulating to the imagination as Tombstone, Arizona Territory. The town's name alone excites visions of wild west activity, but the line-up of personal labels that identify the characteristics of their owners is unique. Names such as Doc Holliday, Big Nose Kate, Curly Bill Brocious, Wyatt Earp, and Ike Clanton are just a few of those names that come to mind when Tombstone is thought of.

How about Johnny Ringo? Now that's a name that sparks one's fancy. And indeed, this man fits the vision that appears. Handsome, brooding, a loner of sorts. Certainly the dangerous suggestion of a dark side that enthralls the romantic notions of most women. But our John Peters Ringo is also an enigma, which makes him even more exciting to the imagination.

Interestingly, and just for the record, his name is Ringo, according to he himself, not Ringgold as some have suggested, thinking Ringo an abbreviation. With that cleared up, now we want to see what else we can find out about this man of mystery.

Almost no one referred to John Ringo as John or Johnny, unless giving his full name. It always seemed to be Ringo, and later, John R. There can be no mistaking who is meant, no confusion between the many Johnny and Johns, a very common name. But the movies have certainly made his name a household word as well as misused it often. They have tweaked his identity to cover such characters as The Ringo Kid, Kid Ringo, Jimmy Ringo and many other imaginative variations. Some of these are, of course, quite misleading. But in the Texas, New Mexico, and southeastern Arizona territories, there was never a misunderstanding.

Ringo's history is rather typical of the time period for a youngster growing up at the height of the great pioneer migrations. His family sought the assurance of a better and more secure future as thousands of others did. There's no real need to go into the moment of birth and what he wore for diapers on the frontier. We can pick up his story much later, and for the truly interested, there are several excellent books available on the life of John Ringo, the latest by David Johnson.

The Ringo family left Liberty, Missouri in 1864. John's mother kept a very accurate diary of the adventure, noting early on in the trip that young John was injured when the wagon ran over his foot. The huge wagons could weigh, unloaded, well over a ton. There's no doubt such an injury would have been quite painful for a period of time. Regardless, it is recorded that John went buffalo hunting with the men the next day. When it came to responsibility, boys were treated as men at a rather young age, often as young as ten or eleven. Being allowed to go on a hunt with the men folk suggested John Ringo was very competent though he was only about fourteen.

There's no doubt that the young man was exposed to various types of violence in his early years due to the fact that the frontier was a tumultuous place at the time. The worst was during the trip west when his father accidentally shot himself when his shotgun went off, literally blowing his brains out. There is no indication the boy saw the fatal accident, but he certainly saw the results, surely having to participate in his father's burial. Can we use this as a basis for his later actions and attitude? Not likely. Trauma of one kind or another was part of life, just as death and hard work were. To say it didn't have an effect would be foolish, but it is unlikely it accounts for his later actions that are regarded as cold and deliberate.

Though many viewed Ringo as a morose and callous individual disenfranchised from his family due to his choices, there is reason to believe this is far from the truth. Apparently both he and his brother left school to help support the family after the death of his father, and John actually remained at home helping until he was about twenty one, an age when most men would have been long gone. However, once the family was secure, he did strike out on his own, only to return to domestic responsibility when learning of his brother's death due to consumption and his mother's unfortunate diagnosis of the same disease. Hardly irresponsible or uncaring, but rather, it demonstrates the finer qualities of loyalty and love, a sense of deep commitment. John's concern for his mother and sisters drove him to Texas where he hoped to get into the cattle business, therefore generating a more substantial income.

The end of the Civil War brought about a time of great upheaval and personal adjustments and it brought John Ringo to Mason County, the sight of the infamous Hoo Doo Wars. He worked and sent money home to sustain his family and had a strong network of friends and associates all eager to make good after the war. He never sought any kind of trouble. As a man of that county the only infractions on his record were disturbing the peace, but what came out of that war changed him. The murders of his friends altered everything in his life at that time and he soon became involved in an exchange of vengeance that was the beginning of his reputation as a dangerous man.

Jailed with Scott Cooley, a notorious badman, freed at the hands of a supportive mob and then let loose throughout the county among reports of continued war casualties, Ringo's celebrity status grew with each newspaper account, whether factual or not. Later, Ringo, charged with murder, languished in jail for the better part of a year, enjoying the company of some of Texas' most notorious gunmen like John Wesley Hardin. Eventually John was released, the case lay in a stack of papers, and, wishing to settle permanently in that county, he actually ran for Constable, winning with a two-thirds majority! ... Only on the Frontier.

Peace and respect at last; yet in no time at all John Ringo was headed west. He headed for the San Simon Cienega, a valley grassland situated between the Peloncillo mountains and Steins Mountain; an area that straddles the New Mexico-Arizona state line. It was here in the mining camp of Gayleyville that John Ringo settled down ... and began to drink heavily.

He did not settle in peacefully, almost immediately becoming involved in a foolish, stupid shooting affair which nearly killed Louis Hancock. Ringo, likely drunk, offered Hancock a whiskey; Hancock preferred beer. The cowboy felt insulted and reacted violently, hitting the man alongside the head with his pistol, the gun going off, perhaps accidentally, perhaps not. John was arrested. The bloody reputation that Ringo left behind him had surfaced and he would be known as a man to be reckoned with in Arizona. It was 1879 and Tombstone was rising out of the desert floor like a canvas phoenix.

But despite his troubles at his own hand, John Ringo wanted to settle in the San Simon valley and filed for a ranch claim between him and Ike Clanton in nearby Animas Valley. Though he had a court case pending, Ringo wrote a very articulate letter to the authorities requesting an extension due to a gunshot injury and explaining that he wished to comply with the law as he hoped to remain in the area permanently. Most of his actions and decisions indicated a course set by a law-abiding cattleman.

Contemporary testimonies from a variety of sources suggest that John Ringo, sober, was an amiable guy. He was admired, respected, and well liked; even a gentleman. But he was a loner of sorts, drank more heavily as time progressed, and unfortunately, was a mean drunk. He drank a lot up in Gayleyville and as a result, became more and more morose, brooding.

In the meantime, the border skirmishes increased, depredations by as many Mexicans as Anglos; stagecoach robberies, cattle rustling and state and federal government confusion and panic. The atmosphere was electric with aggravation of one sort or another, the fire fed by the ambitions of newspapermen who allowed their political objectives to feed the fires that were almost out of control. Ringo managed to get into a little more trouble by robbing a poker game of its purse, though he did return the money when he sobered up, much ashamed of himself. But his name hit the dockets again. His drinking by now was also almost out of control as he found himself in an environment reminiscent of the Mason County War where constant turmoil was the order of the day. The result was the mentality of revenge once again, and Ringo was already programmed for it from past experience.

John Ringo was living in a pressure cooker. The local ranchers were looking to him for leadership. They saw injustice and abuse of power throughout the territory and they needed a champion. Ringo tried to bring the whole thing to a head by openly challenging the Earps to a decisive duel on the streets of Tombstone. They refused, though Doc Holliday was willing. The authorities brought it to a finish and once again, John was charged and fined for carrying a weapon in the city limits. He faced a charge of larceny and looked forward to more court appearances in 1882. Notwithstanding his repeated brushes with the law, John always turned up in court to face his accusers; even when out of the territory he came back to deal with any charges against him when he could have kept going the other way.

But John walked out of court a free man once again and went back to raising cattle, being labeled a "speculator." Only, his demons rode with him, traveling alongside him to Tombstone in July of '82. They provoked him into a heavy drinking spree, an endless bender he couldn't pull out of. Eventually he headed toward home in Gayleyville. His horse knew the way.

Billy Breakenridge ran into him in the Dragoons and described him as *"... very drunk, reeling in the saddle ... it was very hot ... he offered me a drink ... I tasted it ... it was too hot to drink ... it burned my lips ... I tried to get him to turn back with me ... but he was stubborn and went on his way...."*

The next day John Ringo was found dead, an apparent suicide. Much has been made of the way he was found and why his cartridge belt was upside down for example. Why is it so strange and mysterious that a man so drunk he is literally reeling in the saddle would put on a cartridge belt upside down?

The Epitaph wrote a fine obituary. *"...he was recognized by friends and foe alike as a recklessly brave man, who would go any distance, or undergo any hardship to serve a friend or punish an enemy. While undoubtedly reckless, he was far from being a desperado, and we know of no murder being laid to his charge. Friends and foes are unanimous in the opinion that he was a strictly honorable man in all his dealings, and that his word was as good as his bond..."*

What drove John Ringo to sit down in a tree, heave a great sigh, and put his gun to his head ... finally? Could it be he was just tired? Weary of life from the inside out? Yes, I think Johnny Ringo, thirty-two years old, had exhausted himself with the intensity of life and was just tired. It's that simple.

Chapter Nine

Curly Bill Brocious

There is no doubt that many of the itinerant cowboys wandering the rugged southeastern Arizona territories were real bad guys. Certainly some of them were stage robbers, killers, and thieves of every kind. Much like the remnants of every war, these disenfranchised cowboys drifted aimlessly to remote parts of the country where there was little law and order and few concerns about the civilized demands of the developing towns growing out of the dust of the desert. Pima County, later Cochise County, was a veritable paradise for a man whose bent is toward lawlessness or just anonymity.

Some of these boys were left over from the Civil War, the Mason County war, and many other social skirmishes that seemed to grow out of the reconstruction era. Families were scattered, young men desired independence then as now, and many just wanted to strike out as true pioneers, seeking their fortunes through land, gold or silver at a time when such rich ore strikes were in the news daily. For some, success came with hard work; for others, they sought a way that required much less work and seemed to be much more fun.

We are interested this time in William Brocious, aka Curly Bill. We don't need to go into some of the stories about how he got the name 'Curly Bill.' Likely as not, he was either bald or had curly or wavy hair. There is no reference to baldness, so we will assume he had curly hair. Two photos that exist, each claiming to be Bill, show that his hair was quite curly and dark; but neither photo is established. So we will go with the dark curls anyway.

There is almost no solid information as to where William Brocious originated from. The general consensus is Texas, probably because most of his associates were Texans at one time or another. But there seems to be no question that Bill was a real bad guy. Though many of his friends were kind of in-and-out outlaws and rustlers, Brocious seemed to be the real McCoy.

And yet, there is that old bugaboo again! Curly Bill is known to have shot and killed only one man, and that appeared to be an accident at the time. There are suspicions; accusations; not much in the way of established fact.

The first we really hear about William Brocious is in Tombstone in late 1880. A few cowboys were hurrahing the town back of Allen Street along Sixth, a rough section mostly confined to miners and prostitutes. Under the influence of John Barleycorn a few of the boys began shooting their guns off in the air and making a general nuisance of themselves as well as posing some possible danger. Marshal Fred White felt the need to go down and put a stop to the impending trouble and ran into Curly Bill right away. Fred was likely agitated and a little quick, as he assumed Bill was the problem; at least a major part of the problem. Nothing in the reports indicates that Bill had his gun in hand so we can't be sure. But Marshal White demanded the gun, calling Bill an s-o-b. Was Bill drunk? We don't really know that either.

However, it was reported that a mine laborer by the name of Andrew McCauley and another miner from Charleston named James Johnson, who were running from the trouble, actually heard Brocious call out to the others, "This won't do, boys!" Bill then joined the two miners seeking shelter from the flying missiles.

Here accounts differ. Depending on what one you read it is either Wyatt or Virgil Earp who rushed to the assistance of Fred White, coming upon him just as he confronted Curly Bill. White announced himself as an officer of the law and demanded the pistol. Bill obeyed, pulled his pistol from its holster and presented it to the marshal. What happened next also depends on what account you read, but the gist of it is that the gun was presented barrel first, White grabbed at the gun and jerked it from Bill's grasp, and the gun went off. Fred White received the bullet in the groin, damaging the lower intestine. In 1880, there was no way he could survive and death would be painful and slow. Possibly the gun went off because Earp grabbed Curly from behind, wrapping his arms around him so that he was thrown off balance and jerked the trigger. Or, it might well be as Curly said; that his gun had a touchy trigger mechanism and the action caused it to go off regardless of who had hold of it. The results were tragic, though it later turned out that Bill was cleared of a serious charge through the testimonies of Fred White himself. White stated on his death bed that the whole thing was accidental, and the testimony of Wyatt Earp who also stated the shooting was an accident brought about Bill's release. This, of course, suggests the assisting officer had to be Wyatt. It was also noted that there was only one empty shell in Curly's gun, showing he was not one of the revelers shooting up the town.

Curly was rarely seen in the Tombstone vicinity after that initial episode but Fred White's grave marker reads 'murdered by Curly Bill' even today. Though the killing was clearly accidental at that time, Bill began to build a reputation all the same.

To many writers and readers today, Curly Bill seemed to be an outlaw leader of sorts, though I don't get that from what I've read about him. Perhaps he had a charismatic personality or perhaps he had an aura of danger about him that caused others to give him more than his due. I really don't know; but a leader? I'm inclined to think he was not really. Actually, cowboys being the independent cusses they were, it is unlikely any one of the bunch was actually a leader, though some might be better liked than others. But people seem to like the idea of an organized gang with a man at the head doing all the real thinking and planning, and they want to believe it.

Though Curly was a 'hell-raiser' at times as he hung out with a very tough crowd, he seems not to have been anything more than a general nuisance, as were many of the cowboys when they came to town and got drunk. He is known to have caused considerable consternation in Charleston and Contention City when drinking. He 'tore up the town' by shooting up a saloon, forcing the patrons male and female to not only disrobe, but to dance for his entertainment. He also attended the local church services and livened them up considerably, giving the presiding clergyman a clear vision of the near hear-after! Outside of episodes of this nature, some border raiding and cattle stealing, Curly Bill Brocious appears to be just another 'free spirit' enjoying the fruits of his questionable labor.

What Curly Bill is best remembered for is his mysterious disappearance. The enduring question is; did Wyatt Earp really kill Curly, or did he just read the handwriting on the wall and move on down the line as many of his cronies bit the dust? Many believe Wyatt Earp's account about how he and his posse ran across Bill and some of his boys at Iron Springs, a watering hole and stage stop in the Whetstone Mountains. According to Earp, he and his band came across the cowboys unexpectedly and a raging gunfight ensued, Earp shooting Curly with a shotgun blast that almost cut him in half!

Aside from the fact that Wyatt Earp and Baron Munchausen have a great deal in common, I am inclined to question this event as suspect. I have hiked up to Iron Springs (providing the location was correct) and looking around; I had to wonder how this came about in the manner Earp described. The natural spring does bubble out of the ground in front of a rock wall amongst a lot of trees and shrubbery. It sits up on a hillside that affords a pretty good look around the immediate area. There are footprints of several buildings very close by, almost clustered, as well as the occasional parts of corrals that at least indicate where the corrals might have been. If this was a stage stop as believed, the point of arrival for horses and coaches appeared to be rather narrow and a little down in a gulch. I cannot see how the Earp crowd came up on the cowboys unexpectedly, if only because the corralled horses would have indicated the nearness of other horses by pricking their ears and looking in the direction of the new arrivals, and possibly nickering as well. Cowboys know how to read their animals. Not to mention there would be several people living at the stage stop and certainly alert individuals as they were in a remote area in Apache country. No one was napping!

Wyatt Earp describes surprising these frontiersmen who live their lives in the saddle and in the brush, ever aware of the elements around them. As gunfire breaks out, Wyatt's posse makes for cover, leaving him out there, all alone to deal with the whole crowd. But Wyatt is unaware, of course, and stands his ground as bullets fly all around him, miraculously missing him, though some tear through his clothing and his saddle. Even his horse is spared, as big as he is!

After killing Curly Bill with his shotgun, Wyatt & Co ride off. Curly is never heard from again in southeastern Arizona.

However, there are a number of reports following this event, by persons who claimed to know Curly well, that he had left the area much earlier, and that he came through the territory once or twice, stopping to visit old friends. These accounts, for no solid reason, are rejected. Wyatt Earp has had the last word on Curly Bill Brocious for now...but the legend of Curly Bill lives on!

Author's notes: *Frank Vaughn has once again supplied us with a little insight into the ways of the characters around Tombstone with this account; "...the Earps were just bullies. As for them killing Curley Bill, that is not so. Curley was in Mexico when they claimed they shot him. Ten years later Ben Parker and Uncle John Lyons claimed that Curley came to Benson and had dinner with Lew Redfield, that he was living in Mexico and had a wife and family. The Earps were never more than just annoying insects to him and once he slapped one of them down with his open hand..."*

Additional and reliable evidence that Curly Bill did indeed move on down to Mexico, become involved in mining and cattle ranching, as well as establish a family with a number of children has been documented by author and historian Lynn Bailey, who will be releasing such information in his new book. Thank you, Lynn.

Chapter Ten

Major Frink

On October 26th, in the year 1881, three men rode into the town of Tombstone about two o'clock in the afternoon. Tombstone, a mining town in the full bloom of success, was a beehive of swirling energy. The streets were crowded with horses, wagons, people, and the continuous cloud of dust from all the activity. But the three horsemen maneuvered their way through the crowded streets, knowing exactly where they were headed. They dismounted in front of the Grand Hotel, a very classy establishment on Allen Street, between Fourth and Fifth streets, and a favorite stop of many of the local ranchers and cowboys when they came to town for some refreshment after the harsh working conditions of their environment.

But who were these three men? Why are we interested in their arrival in Tombstone on this particular day?

The taller one is the youngest. This is Billy Clanton, younger brother of Ike and Phin Clanton. He is a cowboy and rancher from the San Pedro valley. Though Billy has been accused by the Earp brothers of being a cattle rustler, there has been no evidence to support the claim, which seems to stem from a personal conflict between the two camps.

The other young man with him is Frank McLaury, also a local rancher and close friend. Frank is shorter, darker, and in his thirties. He is well known in the Sulphur Springs valley as a rancher and good neighbor, even though he and his brother are also accused by the Earps as being outlaws and rustlers.

But the third man interests us this time. He is noticeably older than his companions, perhaps in his fifties. As he dismounts, he indicates relief at getting out of the saddle. This man is Major Frink, also a well-respected rancher from the Sulphur Springs valley. He has just finished a round-up of over six hundred cattle. Some were his; some were those of his companions. Yet these three men together raise an interesting question.

The question is, of course, why is this man Frink in close business association with two men who have been suspected of cattle thievery? The answer is in Major Frink himself.

J.R. Frink was a product of his times as were his contemporaries. Today, we make western heroes and exciting and admirable movie characters out of men like him; but in his day, he reflected the qualities and abilities of all the men he dealt with on a daily basis. Tough times breed tough men, yet they were the norm for their day. Frink's background helps us to get a better grasp of him and his associates.

John Randolph Frink originated in St. Louis, Missouri and started right in with a colorful career in history, becoming a dispatch rider for Kit Carson from St. Louis to Albuquerque, New Mexico; no small feat. Later on, he became a wagon master for freight wagon trains across the Great Plains, and this is likely where he earned the title 'Major.' Wagon masters were often appointed the title by the people on the wagon trains and the name usually stuck through a lifetime. He apparently continued his connection with Kit Carson as he had also been in charge of Carson's scouts, earning the title of Captain as a mark of respect. There is no doubt that J.R. Frink was a courageous and effective leader of men.

By the early 1870's he had established himself on a ranch in the San Timoteo Canyon in San Bernardino County, California, which became a favorite stop for overland stagecoach travel, freighting caravans, and travelers of all kinds.

So our Major Frink was a very experienced frontiersman, a family man well established, as well as quite successful financially. As a leader of men and trusted by some outstanding pioneers of American history, one assumes he also is a man who has a keen and discerning eye toward his fellow man. Certainly not a man to be taken in easily. That would be no way to survive on the frontier.

Now, we could go into his resume of many accomplishments, but we are more interested in the kind of man he was and how he dealt with his associates, as this might explain his working relationship with men like the Clantons and McLaurys, as well as give us a clue as to what kind of men they were at the time.

Frink had a ranch in the Sulphur Springs valley near that of the McLaury brothers. He would have known all the cowboys and ranchers in the valley as well as many in neighboring valleys. He was a colorful character to writers, and a hard-nosed, hard working rancher. He had little fear and actually went off single-handedly after some Apache hostiles who had stolen some of his horses. Trailing them under difficult conditions, pouring rain and heavy mud, he retrieved his horses and drove off the hostiles.

Was he an honest man? A relative term on the frontier, especially among start-up ranchers. Did he, like many of his neighbors, use a 'long rope' to build his herd? Very likely. The line was grayed by opportunity, multiple brands, no brands at all, calves not branded though their mothers were, and so on. If a representative cowboy was sent out to locate missing cattle, they would be returned immediately or the price of such cows, had they been sold; but otherwise the 'stolen' cattle would be absorbed into the larger herd with few pangs of conscience. To say everyone was doing it would be an understatement.

Then how did Major Frink, a well-respected rancher and businessman in Cochise County, view his neighbors like the McLaury brothers and their friends the Clantons? Much like himself, I would think. Not as wholesale rustlers, but as men who minded their own business when it came to other men's dealings over cattle. Cowmen were not inclined to judge one another, but would keep their opinions to themselves. However, if a man actually stepped too far over the line, they would wisely curb their association with such a man. Apparently Frink did not view the Clantons and Mclaurys as men who stepped too far over the line, or it would be unlikely that he would enter into a business partnership with either family.

Frink had lived in the San Timoteo canyon in San Bernardino County, California, as did the Clantons for a time. It is most likely they knew each other or at least, of each other, as Major Frink was a prominent man in that area. Apparently whatever Frink knew about the Clantons did not deter him from doing business with them. His association with the McLaurys developed from their being neighbors in the Sulphur Springs valley and likely working together in any number of ways. Interestingly, the Earps had also lived in the San Timoteo canyon at the same time. It appears Frink knew them as well; however, there is no record that he ever supported them.

So then, am I reading too much into Frink's position and his resultant business association with the Clantons and McLaurys? I don't think so. Many of these revealing associations and their statements are frequently 'swept under the rug' in an effort to keep the myth of the Earps' reputation alive and well; the need, then, is to paint all the cowboys and ranchers in the valleys with a broad brush, rendering them unreliable and even untruthful.

That narrow viewpoint needs to change in the interest of true historic understanding.

Chapter Eleven

Sherm McMaster

Another one of history's mysteries! The stories of these many characters that flooded the southwestern sections of the country back in the pioneering days are full of contradictions, half-truths, and complete truths that are almost too hard to believe. The men and women who braved the rugged frontier for any number of reasons left us an incomplete record of their brief passing that fascinates us all the more because we cannot fill in the spaces. However, with what we have, and our power of reason and logic, sometimes we can paint an interesting portrait without straying too far from the accuracy we all long to see.

Such might be the case with the man known to Cochise County as Sherm McMasters.

According to extensive research done by *Peter Brand* of Australia, McMaster's record is a very checkered one and at times quite confusing. One has a difficult time determining if this man is an outlaw, a lawman, or a sometimes line-jumper!

His arrival in Arizona Territory appears to be close to the 1879 time period. *Peter Brand's* diligent sleuthing has turned up evidence that Sherm McMaster was active as a Texas Ranger in El Paso County from September 1st, 1878 until April 12th, 1879.

The transition from lawman to close associate of known outlaws had to be an easy one, as it was for many in those days. The lines seemed blurred at times. Though everyone had to recognize the badge of law, they didn't always recognize the lawless element as easily due to the variety of personalities. But Sherm McMaster chose known bad men like Pony Diehl, an alias for his real name, and Charles Ray, as his companion. This man had gone through his growing pains in the Lincoln County War, such warring factions breeding cowboys turned outlaws through the justification of the cause at the time. Certainly, many of these men did not see themselves as hardened criminals. There was always a reason that a man turned to outlawry, and it wasn't always greed.

Two other friends of McMaster's were Frank Stilwell and Pete Spence, (aka Spencer) both men being constantly in and out of trouble in Tombstone's turbulent historical record. Their names come up frequently. So do the names of Curly Bill Brocious and John Ringo, though Ringo is another enigma, casting a large but light shadow of information regarding his lawless activities.

The first time we really hear about some of these men in association with McMaster in Arizona Territory is during the 'stolen mule account.' The Earp brothers related how they had been tracking some army mules stolen from Camp Rucker, they claiming that they actually trailed the mules as they were being driven by the McLaury brothers. However, when the army Lieutenant posted his reward notice in the Epitaph newspaper, he charged Pony Diehl, A.T. Hansbrough, and Mac DeMasters as the thieves. When Frank McLaury placed a 'card' in response in the paper, he referred to Mac Masters. It appears that there were a number of ways that Sherm McMaster's name could be expressed among his contemporaries.

Amazingly, though McMaster is accused of the crime against the United States Army, there are never any consequences even though he remained at large in the territory, often coming into the towns of Tombstone and Charleston. He was not hard to find!

The next activity of notoriety that we hear about Sherm McMaster is in connection with the robbery of the U.S. Mail from the Globe stagecoach in February of 1881. Our man, along with buddy Pony Diehl, was the suspect for some time, and though indictments seemed to go down easily on a whim, in McMaster's case no action was taken against him for months. Again, he was not hard to find, but it wasn't until Pony Diehl was arrested that anything came of it. Did Diehl sing like a bird, as they used to say in the old gangster movies, ratting on his buddy? Not likely. That was not in the make-up of these frontier characters.

Now, to my mind, here is where the whole story becomes somewhat strange. In the September 10th edition of the *Tombstone Daily Nugget,* the headline read thus; *"Escape of a Highwayman."* It went on to describe an episode in Tombstone involving Virgil Earp, the Marshal, and an escaping stage robber by the name of Sherm McMaster. There was a shot in town and then, after a few moments, several more shots. It seems the lawman had attempted to arrest the rascal and then his man had started to run which caused the Marshal to fire several shots after him.

After some delay, Virgil Earp had finally received a telegram from Bob Paul, the sheriff of Pima County, telling him to arrest McMaster now that Pony Diehl was under wraps. Virgil seemed to attempt to do so, but somehow lost his quarry on the edge of town in the dark. Okay, this is understandable. It was dark and the desert brush was thick.

Strangely enough, McMaster didn't seem to be pursued any further regarding this particular crime, though once again, he was not hard to find, visiting the local towns and saloons as before.

Next, in January of 1882, the Bisbee stage is robbed. There have been a number of stage attacks in between, but apparently not involving our man, McMaster. According to the dictated memoirs of Wyatt Earp, he hired Sherm to spy out suspected stage robbers Curly Bill and John Ringo! He didn't know where to find them? Everyone knew where they were. Ringo had a ranch up in the San Simon valley. He hung out with Diehl and many others in Galeyville. Like many of Earp's stories, this one makes me chuckle. When Ringo had a court date he actually wrote to the court requesting a new date due to a gunshot wound. He wasn't hiding!

And why is Wyatt associating with and hiring a man who is a fugitive from the law; unless, of course, the previous situations were just dropped for unknown reasons? There didn't appear to be any follow-up on the incident regarding the stolen mules, nor any such pursuit over his escaping Virgil Earp, even though Virgil actually shot at the man. Wyatt's undercover man? Perhaps Wyatt was reading those Ned Buntline dime novels too much.

Sherm McMaster also was involved in horse thieving, a serious offense though it seems petty after some of the other accusations. Yet nothing ever really came of these charges. He was allowed to circulate in Tombstone and Charleston openly after running from Virgil Earp, the marshal. Then he was deputized as a posse member. And then the charges against him due to the Globe stage robbery seemed to disappear like smoke. How fortunate can one guy get?

But there's more! Though McMaster is often connected with the rough element of the San Simon crowd, he is as often associated with the Earps. Now, there seems to be two schools of thought regarding this mysterious camaraderie. One, Sherm McMaster is an outlaw who made a conversion to respectability and became a good guy aligned with the Earp brothers, or he is an undercover man for the Earps, spying on the bad men in the Ringo/Curly Bill crowd. Wyatt Earp, in dictating his memoirs to his friend John Flood, said that Sherm McMaster was *"...employed by Earp to ascertain the whereabouts of Curly Bill and Pony Diehl following the January 1882 robbery of the Bisbee stage..."* Once again, it seems rather preposterous. Who did Wyatt ever arrest among the so-called rustlers and stage robbers from the information gathered by McMasters? Just how effective was this subterfuge? Not very. A trip to Galeyville or even Charleston would have turned up almost any of the outlaws being sought, though no one there would have given further direction. Even if Sherm McMaster did tell Wyatt Earp where to find one of these men, Earp would have had to go up to the location himself to affect an arrest, something he could have done in the beginning, because you can bet he knew where all of them were. Where Wyatt's stories surface, I smell a skunk in the woodpile!

McMaster had been a very close buddy of Pony Diehl's almost from the time they arrived in Arizona. It is very unlikely he would turn on Diehl even if he 'went straight.' It was just not the way these men dealt with each other. The whole story from the Earp side seems to be absolute nonsense.

So what is the story behind Sherman McMaster? It is, as I said in the beginning, a mystery. He did seem to evade consequences of his numerous criminal acts, mysteriously. He did associate closely with the Earps and left Arizona Territory with them after they committed several murders. It is interesting that from that point on he seemed to vanish into thin air. He was never tracked, never heard from again, at least not under that name.

His somewhat visible record nevertheless remains a see-saw of controversy. Hopefully, somewhere more will surface; but for now ... Sherm McMaster remains an enigma, as did many others in the Cochise County drama.

Chapter Twelve

Frank Stillwell

The man on the table was soaked in blood from chest to foot, his clothes stuck to his body in places. The Coroner walked around the table several times looking over the condition of the dead man. The legs were angled slightly in an unnatural direction due to broken bones, and the face was distorted in pain. There was little doubt this man had died in great agony and fear. The Coroner shook his head in distaste and began writing in the form he used for the report. In the 1870's and 80's, there were occasionally men brought in, mutilated by Apaches, shot in gunfights, beaten badly for any number of reasons; but this man had been murdered in a most despicable way. Multiple gunshot wounds at very close range by any number of gunmen, both by shotgun and by hand guns. Why the need to attack a single man, obviously unprepared, with such ferocity? His own handgun never left its resting place. What sort of men, even on the wild frontier, would do such a thing?

The Coroner's subject was a man named Frank Stilwell, about twenty-five years old, good looking, well built...and an established businessman from Cochise County. The year is 1882; it is Monday evening of the 20th of March. And the wire services around the country are wild with speculation! Who had done the despicable deed was not in question; but why, and why with such violent cruelty?

Frank Stilwell is also *our* subject. And he, like so many of his contemporaries, presents an enigma once again. The rowdy cowboy element of Cochise County and its surrounding territory seemed to, at times, present legitimate means of livelihood while suddenly appearing to jump off the deep end into some unreasonable short-term career in outlawry! Can we sort this out and find out what is the real situation with Stilwell? Well, we can try!

This young man's background does not infer a life of crime at all. He certainly didn't appear to *need* to choose such a course. The family background was stable and our man started out working as a freighter with his brother Jack. Many sets of brothers started the pioneering movement in the early days of the territory, forging ahead to establish roots for themselves, their future offspring, and even their families left behind. The Stilwell brothers were hard-working young men, teamsters, turning up in Arizona about 1877, before the establishment of the silver strike but about the time many of Tombstone's rural neighbors were getting settled in ranching and farming throughout the San Pedro valley.

Frank chose the budding community of Charleston for his first business venture. Charleston sat on the San Pedro River about nine miles southwest of the site of Tombstone's silver mines, and was later reported to be pretty wild and wooly with little law enforcement. Stilwell invested in a saloon, also selling wholesale liquor, and started a livery stable. These should have been lucrative business interests in a growing community. Certainly the demand for such services was there. Frank should have been fairly comfortable.

The elder Mr. Stilwell held a position as an agent for the Tombstone-Bisbee stage company in the mining town of Bisbee, about 26 miles south of Tombstone. In 1880, still apparently successful in Charleston, Frank decided to relocate to Bisbee. There he and a friend by the name of Pete Spence partnered in another saloon effort. At the same time, Frank was appointed a deputy sheriff for Tombstone sheriff Johnny Behan. So it seems fair to assume that Frank had a more than adequate income in an area that was literally 'the land of opportunity' for an enterprising young man.

But, darn it! There's the rub! During all this activity, our man was also involved in a number of scrapes with the law. In 1877, he shot a man named Jesus Bega up in the Prescott area. The court pronounced him innocent, so possibly it was an altercation between two men that we will know nothing about. But these were tough times with tough men and these types of confrontations happened pretty often. However, it got more serious in 1879, as Frank was involved in an actual killing at his Brunckow mine; a man named J.W. Houghton. Again, no real information, but Frank was cleared.

For the time period, we can recognize that such episodes happened. There is no explanation as to who was the aggressor. But the next arrest makes us wonder about this young man. It appears that he and Pete Spence, his business partner and friend, robbed the Bisbee stage in September of 1881. At least, that is what Wyatt Earp arrested them for. The evidence against them seemed reasonable, yet nothing came of it, except that there was a follow-up indictment for attempted robbery of the U.S. Mail during the same robbery. One has to wonder why such a man, his friend Spence included, felt the need to rob a stage coach. Both men had several business interests, apparently successful. Pete Spence had invested in the very plushy Vogan's saloon in Tombstone, and had some mining interests. He also had a wood cutting business, running several camps with a number of employees. These men were not paupers!

Their escapades and associates put them on a collision course with the Earps for some reason; possibly resentment over the arrest for the Bisbee stage robbery. It was never established as to whether or not they were actually guilty.

But one evening, about 11:00 pm on March 18, 1882, while enjoying a lively game of pool at Campbell & Hatches' saloon, Morgan Earp was shot in the back. The shots came from the back door windows and the assassin was gone in a flash, disappearing into the dark alley behind the saloon in almost any direction. Within an hour, the younger Earp brother was dead from his wounds and the search was on for the attacker.

Frank Stilwell, his friend Pete Spence, and two other men hurried into the home of Spence shortly after the assassination attempt. They were in an agitated state and all armed with rifles and pistols. Clearly, to Marietta Spence, Pete's wife, and her mother, the men were up to no good. They were excited and nervous and left after a bit. Marietta testified at the Coroner's jury regarding this strange state of affairs, stating that she was sure Pete and his friends were involved even though they never said so, but Pete had threatened her to keep her mouth shut about the night's activities.

It seems that Marietta's sole testimony was the evidence against Pete and Frank regarding the murder of Morgan Earp. Not much more is known as to supporting testimony, so Frank and Pete, along with Indian Charlie and a man named Freis were the men suspected of the killing. Yet there is always a question in my mind where these fellows are concerned. Not everything adds up as it should.

There has been much discussion in many books about how Frank Stilwell could have killed Morgan Earp around 11:00 pm. in Tombstone and then sign in at a hotel in Tucson at 5:00 am the next morning, Tucson being a good seventy-five miles away over rough terrain. No horse could do that in that time period. It meant uphill, through rocky terrain for much of the way. Stage companies traded horses every ten miles or so and still lost some because of the grueling work load. Then, it has been suggested that he might have caught the Emigrant train that could have gotten him to Tucson sometime early morn.

The question seems to be, *could* he have done it rather than *did* he do it. It seems that Frank was in Tucson with Ike Clanton for the purpose of answering subpoenas to appear before the Grand Jury in a case pending against a friend by the name of Jerry Barton. As Frank was in Tucson for the court case and he and Ike had gone down to the railroad station to meet another witness, it seems unlikely that he was aware of the Coroner's Jury and its indictment against him. Especially as the train that came in was loaded with Earps! Would he not realize, had he actually snuffed Morgan, that a trainload of Earps meant serious trouble for him? Ike left the station because, once realizing the Earps were at the station, Stilwell warned Ike to leave as he felt Ike was in danger. Why did he not see himself in danger? Apparently, Frank did not feel he was in a threatened position because he made no attempt to flee the area. It is a real mystery and makes little sense in the way the story is accepted.

At any rate, the Earp bunch spotted Frank, chased him down in the dark, and shot him at close range, apparently several of the men in the group shooting into what had to very quickly be a dead body. The attack was sick and vicious. These men had no proof that Frank Stilwell had actually killed Morgan, just as they had no proof that Ike Clanton or Pete Spence had been directly involved.

The Coroner finished his report. The consensus was that Frank was the *'worst shot-up man I've ever seen!'* Frank was buried immediately in an unmarked grave in Tucson's old cemetery and quickly forgotten. But what was the true story about Frank Stilwell? Did he kill Morgan Earp late at night and then turn up in Tucson five or six hours later? Or was he in Tucson already? But Marietta Spence said he was at her house with Spence the night of Morgan's murder. Like so many of the characters that round out the Tombstone saga, Frank has left us a conundrum. An energetic entrepreneur and successful businessman at a young age and yet a stage robber with apparently no monetary need to turn to robbery, who has gotten involved with suspected murder and a most unnerving end.

Hopefully, someone will enlighten us with new-found information someday that will answer the endless questions.

I should include here a big thanks to Kenny Vail for the use of an original photo of Pony Diehl from which this drawing was created. Thank you Kenny!

JA

Chapter Thirteen

Pete Spence

In the early days of our country the frontier, though fraught with dangers from both man and beast, provided many advantages as well. Anonymity was certainly one of them. A man could move on no more than a couple of hundred miles, change his name.... and change his life! Transportation was slow and expensive, if not arduous. Communication was still developing, though at a relatively rapid pace, but each of these slowed the progress of following up on anyone. Most important; people did not ask a lot of questions. So, for the man who might have made a few mistakes, accidentally or deliberately, a new environment was welcome and not too hard to attain if he wished to leave his bad memories behind him.

Such was the case for Pete Spence; woodcutter, cowboy, lawman, stage robber, Ranger, saloon keeper, rustler, deputy sheriff, and all-around opportunistic character. With a few aliases trailing behind him, Pete landed in the middle of the Tombstone saga with a thud!

For a great deal of information on Pete Spence I will be relying on historical research collected by Roy Young. I make mention of his book, *"Pete Spence; Audacious Artist in Crime,"* so that the reader who wishes to know more about Pete and many of his associates can enjoy this very informative work. The footnotes alone are a Who's Who of southeastern Arizona rascals.

When Pete Spence showed up in Arizona about 1878, he immediately lost the anonymous standing he sought by becoming involved in a murder. So our man was not successful in starting off with a clean slate! Murder was just the beginning in this neck of the woods, and though he walked away when a jury freed him due to lack of evidence, he apparently didn't benefit from his fortunate situation.

By now you want to know who Pete Spence is and why are we interested in him. Simply put, he was one of the outlaw element that the Earp brothers claimed to deal with during their exciting days in Tombstone. Actually, he was a key player. Wyatt Earp had made the comment in an interview with a Colorado newspaper reporter that "...I would sooner have met him than any s-o-b..."

But why? Well, it seems Wyatt Earp believed that Spence was a part of the assassination attempt on his brother Virgil, an attempt that Virgil survived. And Wyatt also believed that Spence was involved in the murder of his brother Morgan, each of these shootings in retaliation for the killings of three ranchers at the vacant lot on Fremont Street near the OK corral.

Though he looked for Pete Spence at the time with the intention of killing him, Earp didn't find Pete. Yet, years later, when he was in an advanced age, Wyatt told Stuart Lake, his biographer, that he no longer believed that Spence was one of the men who attacked his brothers. Great! What would have happened if Wyatt had found Pete at the time, as there was almost no evidence to support Wyatt's assumptions? Wyatt and his group would have killed an innocent man.

So how bad a man was Pete Spence and could he actually have been a serious threat to the Earp brothers? What was his background and where did he come from?

Without digging too deep, it appears our man was originally known as Lark Ferguson, possibly born and raised in Texas. During the early 1870's he served as a Texas Ranger for a short while, albeit with a group that had a reputation for being a renegade company of lawmen. The frontier in Texas during this time was a very dangerous place and the Rangers apparently adjusted their methods accordingly. Surely that was a start toward violence in the life of Lark Ferguson.

For the following two years in Texas, Lark Ferguson wrecked havoc; horse stealing, killing, and bank robbery. His name was well known. As his reputation preceded him, it was time to move on!

The amazing thing about these guys is how they easily mixed legitimate business with their outlaw escapades; one has to wonder why! Pete Spence formed a close association with a fellow named Frank Stilwell, a man who originally had a good background. He also had a saloon, a livery, a wood yard and some other interests in the town of Charleston, a favorite hangout of a number of notorious characters. Charleston sat on the banks of the San Pedro River, a mill town with little law and order, but a bustling little center of activity for local miners and ranchers. Apparently Frank Stilwell was doing quite well.

And so was Mr. Spence, who had several wood cutting camps and employees in the Dragoon Mountains. But wood cutting and hauling is hard work, so perhaps Pete was tired already of common labor, no matter how lucrative it might have been. At any rate, for some reason, he and Frank hit it off and developed a 'business' relationship. In no time at all, they were into bigger and better things.

Mr. Spence and Mr. Stilwell soon became mining partners, though neither one had any known experience in such a venture. However, they did strike it rich! Beginner's luck? Perhaps, but the strike did support them for a couple of years.

Interestingly, Pete also purchased a house in Tombstone, a house that still stands today, sadly neglected though it is one of the oldest homes in town and a truly historic site. This house stands on the southeast corner of First and Fremont, unknown and closed to the public. It was also owned at one time by Newman 'Old Man' Clanton. It should be recognized.

But now Pete Spence continued his legitimate enterprise by purchasing Vogan's Saloon, a very classy establishment. One wonders why Pete Spence and Frank Stilwell, both doing fairly well by this time, turned their attention to Bisbee and the possibility of scoring a big stage robbery!

The two desperadoes did indeed hold up the Bisbee stage and were arrested for it, the circumstances too lengthy to relate here. They were suspects in other stage robberies but never indicted. However, many believe that their arrest by the Earp brothers actually touched off a 'cowboy war,' involving the McLaurys, the Clantons, John Ringo, Curly Billy Brocious, Joe Hill and numerous others. Though all these men associated with one another to a greater or lesser degree, unless there is something we don't know about today, it seems unlikely that any of these men would declare war over Spence and Stilwell being arrested for something they obviously were guilty of. Cowboys didn't usually butt into others' affairs and usually expected each man to 'carry his own load'; be accountable for his own actions. The onset of a cowboy war sounds a lot like the Earp side of the story, which is always questionable.

During the famous street fight between the Clantons and Mclaurys and the Earp faction, both Pete and Frank Stilwell were in jail. But in the ensuing months, volatile events incorporated the names of these two men as co-conspirators in the attempted assassination of Virgil Earp and the successful murder of Morgan Earp. Wyatt Earp became convinced that both men were involved and during his famous 'vendetta' ride in which he and his supporters sought out suspected murderers and executed them; they did shoot and kill Frank Stilwell. They were unable to locate Pete Spence at the time and immediately had to leave the Territory under issued murder warrants for Wyatt and his posse of avengers.

Pete's narrow escape did nothing to improve his attitude. Over the years he was involved in a number of killings, mostly Mexicans, which he claimed to hate even though his wife was Mexican. Pete eventually was sentenced to five years in Yuma prison, a brutal time period which is said to have broken his health. In reality, it appears that the Texas bad man suffered a broken spirit, failing daily, even though he served only fifteen months of his five year sentence. Pete applied for and received a pardon in 1894.

Where does a broken-hearted outlaw go when it's all over? How does such a one retire? One last hurrah, shooting up a saloon or a stagecoach? Not at all! The accepted belief is that Pete Spence went down to old Mexico and spent a few years there. Later, he relocated up in the Globe area, connecting with an old crony, Phineas Clanton. Phin had a ranch up that way, was married, and raising goats as well as dabbling in a little mining. He had a bad accident when his team ran away and the wagon overturned, the resulting injuries believed to be the eventual cause of his death. His friend Pete inherited the ranch, the goats, and apparently the wife!

Assuming that Pete Spence appreciated the good cooking that Phin had enjoyed, Pete married Phin's widow not too long after Phin passed on. He also raised goats and lived a quiet life on Clanton's ranch. He died of pneumonia at age 72, quietly going out without a bang. He was buried in an unmarked grave next to his friend, Phin Clanton, in the Globe cemetery.

However, if Wyatt Earp would have found him at the time he was seeking vengeance, Pete's story would have been much shorter. But then, a whole lot of Mexicans would have gone on to marry, raise families, and possibly be successful goat ranchers too!

Chapter Fourteen

The Mavericks

There were many cowboys, ranchers, saddle tramps, drifters and outright hard case outlaws throughout Cochise County, both in its earliest days as Pima County and when it was realigned as Cochise. As we have looked over a few of the better known names, we were surprised to find that some of them were self-sufficient financially and didn't appear to need to break the law to supplement their bank accounts. They leave us scratching our heads in wonderment; could they just be reckless and adventuresome?

Were things that simple on the frontier for those who survived the Civil War and its devastating aftermath? What happened to so many men who were disengaged after the war? Can we understand the times and the results to these many soldiers, families, friends, townships?

Would it be appropriate to compare these experiences with those of our Viet Nam veterans of the twentieth century? Are the effects of war the same despite the times? The horrors of war don't change; the trauma is still to the individual and the effects are long -lasting. Perhaps the difference is that the Civil War took place in everyone's field and farm, destroyed the roots of a nation to some degree. What became of the thousands of men who could not go home again?

On the other hand, we do not want to use the war experience and the Reconstruction era, when so many communities of families were dislodged from their background, as an excuse for crimes committed. But there was, at the same time, a reshuffling of power between ambitious merchants, wealthy and powerful ranchers and landowners, north and south sympathizers and aimless opportunists with no loyalties all thrown into the unstable mix.

From this explosive and emotional combination emerged some of the rougher elements of our cowboys of southeastern Arizona Territory.

We have already looked into short biographies of the more recognized names that rounded out the colorful and complex pattern of personalities scattered like tumbleweeds throughout the area; some anchored and others forever caught in the shifting winds. But there were also the larger and more respected ranchers that maintained a tight foothold throughout the three valleys. The Vail brothers, Henry Hooker, John Slaughter; these were some of the ranchers whose size protected them. However, one must not get the idea that property and money represented a more moral group. Such assets were acquired on the frontier at the same cost as the smaller rancher paid- run-ins with Apaches, outlaws, opposing neighbors, border ruffians, and of course, the law. It took rough and reckless cowboys, hired for their willingness to ride for the brand at all costs, as well as their ability with rope, spur, and gun, to keep such cattlemen in power. Though those tactics often lead to bloody range wars, such men made no apologies.

But what about the smaller ranchers, the farmers and the homesteaders? Did they employ such methods? Could they? Likely they did, but their efforts were more contained. And because their struggles to establish themselves were smaller in scope, they were more visible, more exposed to scrutiny. But they became the independent cowboys and small ranchers living by their own code of behavior; mavericks.

Joe Hill was one of these. Like John Ringo, he had had enough of the Hoo Doo war of Mason County, Texas, and relocated in a new environment, western New Mexico. Joe had changed his name from Olney to Hill in order to start fresh in New Mexico about 1877. He then moved his family down into Mexico, buying a ranch near Nueva Casa Grandes, near Corralitos. Joe was one of the few cowboys of that time that had a wife and a number of children. He was very much attached to his family and cared for them responsibly. His brothers were close to him as well and they joined in the ranching efforts in Mexico.

Though Joe Hill's name would be always linked with outlawry there seems to be little to suggest his connection with cattle rustling or crimes attached to the 'cowboys' that were considered a gang of rustlers and stage robbers in southern Arizona; uniquely Cochise County. By that time, Joe Hill seemed to be living and working legitimately. Joe settled further up the Sulphur Springs valley into the San Simon Cienega, near Gayleyville. There, his friend John Ringo, along with Ike Clanton, established a ranch earlier. Quite a number of men began ranching in that lush grassland, ideal for fattening up cattle before market.

So was Joe Olney/Hill actually a cattle rustler? A highwayman? He raised cattle on his own ranch in Mexico and drove them up to the San Simon to prepare them for market. It doesn't seem he was in the rustling business, though he may have taken advantage of opportunities to bypass the border tariff, or pick up a generous amount of strays along the route. Yet all his close friends were men like Ringo, the Clantons, the McLaurys, Pete Spence, Frank Stilwell, and the Patterson brothers. All carried reputations of lawlessness, whether deserved or not.

And there surfaces another name that will show up in reading about the Cochise County desperados; the Patterson brothers. Not too much information is available about them but their name pops up from time to time in connection with the McLaury brothers and the Clantons. They apparently were neighbors of the McLaurys along the Babocomari River to the west of Charleston in the late 1870's. It was Frank Patterson who dealt with Lieutenant Hurst and the Earp posse when the mule incident took place, (see 'In Defense of the Outlaws' by Joyce Aros) he holding the mules on the McLaury ranch. From that incident came the view that a feud had started between the cowboys and the Earps.

Frank Patterson, more so than his brother, had a reputation as a hell-raiser and a bully, his name coming up often in reports of violence in the Tombstone district. Frank was involved in a shooting spree on

Allen Street on October 27, 1880 as well as reported to be involved, along with Frank Stilwell, in the Houten murder at the Brunckow mine in November of 1879.

Little else is known about the Pattersons except that they kept a rather low profile after the Earp/cowboy troubles were over.

But we have not run out of colorful characters! How about Pony Diehl? He was another associate of the above named men, one who seemed to be trying to start over again after escaping jail in Texas. His real name was Charles Ray. This man was also one of those named as a thief regarding the army mules stolen from Camp Rucker and found later on the McLaury ranch. His accomplices were Sherm McMasters and a man named Hansbrough. So much for a clean slate! Diehl seemed to find trouble in Arizona as he had in Texas. He later was arrested along with Phin Clanton in connection with the attempted assassination of Virgil Earp in early 1882. Both men were set free when the evidence against them was recognized as inconclusive. It seems that Phin Clanton might not have been involved. Surely a rifle would have been his weapon of choice rather than a shotgun as he was said to be such a good shot that he only took one bullet with him whenever he went hunting. Had he been involved, its unlikely Virgil would have survived.

So there we have them. A little background, however slight, to give us a look at some of the names that spring from the pages of the Tombstone saga. For so long they have been shadow figures, just names with no personalities or character traits to distinguish them one from another. Hopefully this short series has helped to round out the cast of characters so that the over-all story would be much more interesting. Some of these men came from violent backgrounds yet attempted to leave it behind and start over. For those, the frontier still demanded much of them if they were to survive. Others drifted into the area and found the lack of tight law enforcement exactly what they were looking for. Some, though, confound us with the lack of logical behavior when their circumstances would have spared them conflict with their fellow man and the law.

Yet, is not that the mystique of the old west that intrigues us so? If we had all the answers, would we not go on to new interests? We don't have all the answers; we don't understand it all, nor are we able to fully understand the life of a frontiersman of the nineteenth century.....not with our twenty-first century mentality and moral conflicts. But oh, how we do admire them for what they contributed to our history and yes, to our entertainment.

Who were these men? They were ranchers, cowboys, frontiersmen, and even outlaws that in one way or another contributed to the expansion of the western plains and desert, settling it under some of the most unimaginable hardships.

Here's to the American cowboy, regardless of which side of the law he was on!

THE + END

INDEX

ABOUT THE AUTHOR

Joyce Aros came to Tombstone several times as a teenager back in the 1950's. Much of Allen Street was boarded up and Boothill was a windswept and neglected old cemetery; no fence, no buildings, and few graves still marked with rusty pipes that had worn and dried up pieces of wood wired to them. But it haunted anyone who saw it and beckoned them to return and seek out the stories that were buried there.

Back in Canada, Joyce read everything she could about Tombstone and its fascinating people. Not only the Earps and Doc Holliday, but so many more. However, it soon became apparent that much of it was fiction. The Earp brothers were too good to be true and the cowboys were shadowy figures with no identity.

Years later, after relocating to Tucson, Arizona, Joyce married a working cowboy, one of the last of the old time Vaqueros in the area and got to know a lot of people who still lived a frontier type life. These people were still pioneering in so many ways and still adhered to the old way of living with the land.

Joyce's interest in the characters of the Cochise County exploits was set aside for a few years to raise seven children. But once that was done, it was time to seriously look into the history and find out who really were these men and women of a long time ago.

Not surprisingly, they turned out to be far more interesting than even she imagined. The results were a series of articles published in the Tombstone Times History and Information Journal in defense of the ranchers and cowhands of Cochise County and a continuing search for the true account of the shoot-out at the O.K. Corral, as it has been referred to.

NOTES

NOTES

THE COCHISE COUNTY COWBOYS

Who Were These Men?

by Joyce Aros

You may purchase additional copies of this book from:

Goose Flats Publishing

P.O. Box 813

Tombstone, Arizona 85638

(520) 457-3884

www.gooseflats.com

DEALER INQUIRIES WELCOME

GOOSE FLATS PUBLISHING   TOMBSTONE ~ ARIZONA